PITCH
PERFECT

JOHN LEACH AND JOHN MOON

PITCH PERFECT

Feel the Impact of a Winning Sales Approach

CAPSTONE

First published 2003 by
Capstone Publishing Ltd (a Wiley Company)
The Atrium
Southern Gate
Chichester
West Sussex PO19 8SQ
England
www.wileyeurope.com

CIP catalogue records for this book are available from the British Library and the US Library of Congress

ISBN 1-84112-581-4

Typeset by Forewords, 109 Oxford Road, Cowley, Oxford

Printed and bound by T.J. International Ltd, Padstow, Cornwall

This book is printed on acid-free paper responsibly manufactured from sustainable forestry in which at least two trees are planted for each one used for paper production.

Substantial discounts on bulk quantities of Capstone Books are available to corporations, professional associations and other organizations. For details contact John Wiley & Sons: tel. (+44) 1243 770441, fax (+44) 1243 770517, email corporatedevelopment@wiley.co.uk

Contents

Acknowledgement

A special thank you to Iain Leslie for his support in putting together *Pitch Perfect*. The phone calls, emails and constant discussion did the job – cheers mate!

Foreword

I have spent many years helping businesses create winning cultures through deploying inspirational leadership and catalysing innovative and sustainable change initiatives. My messages are simple, down to earth, practical and most of all effective. When I read *Pitch Perfect* I felt inspired by the pragmatic approaches that these guys are proposing. This book is not for the faint hearted, it's for those individuals that want to make a difference. If you are not wanting to lose, then this is *not* the book for you, if you really do want to win, then you are in exactly the right place. Read on!

It's for high performing organizations that are not interested in just meeting sales targets, but exceeding them. Every sale achieved will take you one step closer to realizing the overall vision for your corporation.

Business is faster and more unforgiving than it has ever been. Being polite, apologetic and passive gets you nowhere in a hurry, whilst the competition is 'taking no prisoners' you may start to feel the kitchen has got just a little too hot for you. If so, it's time for *Pitch Perfect*! To win in today's competitive marketplace we have to be completely 'hard wired' into customer needs and desires. We have to approach customers with fresh thinking and brave ideas that create differentiation, add value and produce long lasting relationships. Gone are the days of the 'me too' practices. You must escape the pull of the past, and think and behave a little differently. You may not have a choice; time is no longer just the enemy, it is now an assassin. Approaches to selling are constantly evolving and everybody in the organization has a part to play in the sales war. Smart businesses are rationalizing and saving costs from the back office in order to invest in the front office – the sales team. As with anything worth doing on any business, the leadership, inspiration and role models all come from the top. If sales are not important to the Chief Executive and their team, why should they be important to anyone else in the company? The CEO is also the CSO; the Chief Sales Officer!

The unique combination of great technique, first-class marketing and the personal touch is a winning combination. *Pitch Perfect* is an easy and enjoyable read, and makes perfect sense. Remember, second place is the first of the losers!

Rene Carayol

SECTION ONE

WELCOME TO PITCH PERFECT

CHAPTER I

Introduction

So – why the book?

Even more so, what's all this stuff about Pitch Perfect? . . . Especially when there's been a plethora of titles over the last few years covering the whole spectrum of sales, marketing and general business and personal improvement.

The reality is that a science has sprung up around these themes, and the shelves of bookshops are full of groundbreaking hypotheses. How easily applied, though, is all this new thinking?

Getting under the skin of much business development theory is by no means straightforward. Making sure that the lessons are absorbed and then applied effectively is even more of a challenge.

In our experience, many businesses struggle to produce sustained levels of improved performance using these innovation tools. Frequently, this is because simple ideas have been overcomplicated. Many of us now live in a world where information overload is rapidly approaching.

Every industry needs its own jargon and model theories, and, as management consultants, we're as culpable as the rest! After all, this "code" is the shorthand that we all use to move swiftly through the day's workload.

What *is*, however, becoming an increasing problem is where we make life difficult for ourselves, and where we end up drowning in theories that are often so far removed from reality that their effective implementation is limited.

What's becoming key, therefore, is being able to sift out and implement the most useful business and management innovations quickly and effectively.

From our perspective, professionals working within the business development arena continue to search for practical, tried and tested advice that solves their everyday problems. We've worked for the last twenty years in a wide range of markets and industries, so the thinking that underpins Pitch Perfect has been shaped through coaching thousands of managers, directors and leaders and showing them how to maximize the effectiveness of their customer identification and acquisition strategies.

WHY WINNING IS IMPORTANT

Winning new customers is one of the most challenging aspects facing businesses today.

Increased competition, both domestically and internationally, means that it's imperative that we stay ahead of the game by constantly adding value and providing creative, customer-centric solutions.

Winning and retaining business should be the key drivers of all organizations. Nothing happens until a sale has been made. No wages can be paid; no new investments made; no human resources or management improvement initiative can be launched. Healthy sales nourish and energize. But while this is something of an obvious point to make, many organizations stumble at the first hurdle.

SOUNDS FAMILIAR?

In writing this book we wanted to share our own experiences and offer some practical guidelines and advice on how you can improve your business development performance.

Pitch Perfect is for everyone working in business that thinks that . . .

- Their growth could be better
- Their sales skills could be improved
- Their customer base could be expanded

It's also for the professional who can identify with some (or all!) of these thoughts . . .

- You often wonder whether you really understand the full market potential for your offer
- A contract was won by a competitor - and you didn't even know it was up for grabs
- You're finding it difficult to get a meeting with key decision makers
- You always feel like you're talking to audiences that appear distinctly uninterested
- You didn't quite address the prospect's needs
- You keep losing contracts that you thought were in the bag
- Your quotations never seem to hit the mark

In this book we aim to share with you how you can improve your own business development performance, because, after all, the two key components to corporate growth and sustainability are effective business development and customer retention.

SELF-MOTIVATION IS VITAL, TOO

Sustaining a positive work attitude and approach when setbacks occur is often very difficult. However, if we took more time to think about what we were doing and how we could refine the approaches that we took towards our prospective customers, then our failure rate would fall.

Learning how to deal with challenges and motivating ourselves to keep things in perspective is a lesson we all have to learn. Those who succeed get back on their bikes when they fall off and pedal even harder. Remember, there's a lot of truth in the old saying 'the harder I try the luckier I get'.

In this book we've considered all the issues that can lead to you identifying, approaching, securing and maintaining a growing customer base – and given you some thoughts that will help you build your resilience.

Much of what is covered in Pitch Perfect is about understanding the subtle interactions between people and what motivates and satisfies these relationships. Successful business development hinges on our ability to ensure others' expectations are met and exceeded, and, put simply, that their hard earned cash has been wisely spent.

IT'S DOWN TO YOU

The bottom line is that a major part of any company's success is the ability of its people to win new business and retain its existing customers – and, as this is probably the most important element of your role, it's down to you!

You control your own destiny and it is up to *you* to make the difference. No excuses. No buck-passing. No tough luck stories.

Pitch Perfect is about *you* getting yourself ready for the challenges that face you, and finding innovative ways of securing customers.

Business development is changing. The real winners out there understand how to scope their market potential effectively. They're able to differentiate and prioritize between hot prospects and time wasters. They're able to make their offer unique because they possess an ability to empathize with the prospect's needs. They're able to convert then keep close to their customers because they ultimately understand that it's about providing solutions to their problems. It's down to you to equip yourself with these talents, but we hope you'll find this book stimulating to help you secure these skills so that you achieve your goals with confidence and vitality.

CHAPTER 2

Business Development Success

THE DRIVING FORCE OF A SUCCESSFUL BUSINESS

Hands up if you think that business development people don't possess the best reputation in the world.

If you've just put your arm in the air, don't worry, you're not alone!

The truth is, however, that although the sales individual is often still thought of as the stereotypical brush seller with their foot firmly wedged in the door, times are changing rapidly.

In our experience, the more innovative businesses and their sales people now rightly deserve to be re-branded as business development professionals. This new breed is emerging as both a problem solver and solution provider. They're not content to regurgitate messages about features and benefits at the lowest price to anyone they think might be worth targeting.

Instead, they're moving in an environment where they spend time working out how their market operates and who their commercially critical prospects are. They then focus on how they can add value by gathering extensive customer data, developing, then proposing suitable options.

Consultative selling is the norm in pioneering industries and sectors today. The business developer's approach focuses less on imposing themselves and their company's offer on clients; instead, it concentrates on offering a toolkit of solutions that make commercial sense for the customer.

The best companies focus on the Selling Process

A survey of CEOs of 402 product and service companies identified in the media as the fastest growing US businesses over the last five years was conducted. The surveyed companies range in size from approximately $5 million to $100 million in revenue/sales. It identified that '81% had over the previous three years initiated important new programmes aimed at customer expansion, retention and profitability. Those planning new customer-focused programmes have achieved 46% faster revenue growth than their peers over the past five years and are projecting a further 35% higher growth over the next 12 months. *PricewaterhouseCoopers' Trendsetter Barometer*

The best business developers, as we will go on to see, don't even think about needing to overcome objections. Preparation and consultation, married to the skills of problem solving, and then getting under the skin of what customers are trying to achieve within given financial parameters become their true keys to success.

It's our view that mastering the skill of business development is one of the most important components of a successful company. It's also our opinion that it is one of the techniques most lacking in corporate life today.

This deficit is especially sharply defined for new start-ups and SMEs. A failure to integrate business development as a core commercial strategy, low confidence levels, lack of knowledge and direction, and poor use of sales techniques means that many businesses never achieve their full potential. This is an even bigger issue when you consider that Springboard, the venture capital company, identified that of the key characteristics that marked out new start-ups as winners, the ability to make *early* sales was the most crucial.

POINTERS TO SUCCESS

Before we share with you our foundation for success it is worth pointing out that there are two primary themes to success in Business Development.

These themes marry practical selling skills with the acquisition of core personal competencies.

Theme 1 – the tools of the trade

There are a number of tried and tested sales tools that can assist us to do our job better.

Market research & intelligence, database management, questioning techniques, presentation aids and brochures are all tools of the business developer's trade. Learning how and when to use them are competencies that we must develop.

Theme 2 – personal development

Using the tools of the trade in isolation is pointless if you don't possess the appropriate social skills.

The best brochures or PowerPoint presentations are useless if the person driving them can't communicate, build relationships or can't – metaphorically, at least! - be bothered to get out of bed. Balancing the tools of the trade with inner personal development is equally crucial for success.

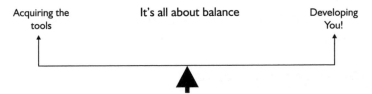

We've worked with thousands of businesses helping them to improve their market share and sales performance. Those companies and individuals that enjoy sustained levels of high performance have three things in common.

Business Development Success = Functional Mastery × Customer Connectivity × Momentum

Although this equation might look like a typical piece of management-speak it's really only common sense.

Here's how the equation works.

First – do you understand fully what your offer can do?

Second – can you effectively engage in a sensible dialogue with the right prospects?

Third – do you genuinely possess drive and energy, and do feel good about yourself and believe in what you are saying?

EXPRESSED AS A SIMPLE EQUATION – THE THREE PRINCIPLES

Achieving business development success through the application of the Pitch Perfect equation revolves around the interdependency of each activity and the fact that each of these three elements needs to be working in harmony and balance with the others.

To truly maximize our chances of success we must be firing on all three cylinders to get the desired effect. Remember the old maths lesson at school? Anything multiplied by zero equals zero, so if we're ticking only two boxes within the equation we're ultimately not going to secure the business development success we're pursuing.

See the connection?

As each element of the equation is vitally important, let's take a closer look:

I KNOW WHAT IT'S ALL ABOUT

Principle 1 – functional mastery

The key to Functional Mastery is: making sure that you fully understand your offer.

What makes what your business does better than the next company?

Can you talk authoritatively about what you've got?

Do people really enjoy meeting with you to discuss how your company's product or service can help them?

Successful business developers enjoy relationships with buyers because they talk authoritatively and help them solve their problems.

"Solve someone's problem and you have a friend for life."

Think about a positive experience when you've really wanted to

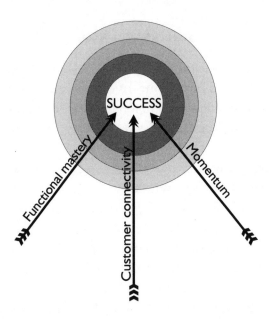

buy something; a new car, or a music system, or whatever. Wasn't part of the fun engaging in discussion with the sales person who really knew what they were talking about?

Functional mastery is the art of developing this capability so that the prospective buyer needs and wants to talk to you because you know how to improve their performance.

Excellence in business development is highly dependent on the ability to solve a buyer's problem, because, after all, most people want an easy life, and your prospect is no different.

MAKING A CONNECTION

Principle 2 – customer connectivity

What do we mean by this term? Well, it's an attempt to demonstrate that to be successful in business development we must acquire the skills of engagement with prospects and make a connection with them.

The golden rules of successful connectivity hinge on three fundamentals:

Find → Win → Keep

An ability to seek out prospective customers and markets is the starting point in any connectivity process. In simple terms, we must find sensible things to tell them and win the battle with a reasoned debate about how you and your offer will meet their needs.

The task, however, doesn't finish here. It's at least three times more expensive to win a new customer than it does to keep an existing one happy. It's crucial, then, to employ strategies that ensure that converted prospects – in other words, customers! - keep coming back for more.

It's a truism, but profitability will grow and orders will keep coming in if customers are looked after.

Customer connectivity builds on the simple principles that:

- The right people have been approached
- They are approached in a manner that they can see real benefit in talking to you
- You can engage and talk authoritatively about your organisation, its products and services
- You can diagnose their needs and provide effective solutions that can often make them look good in the process
- You present your case in a cohesive and lucid manner
- You ask questions that are pertinent and that demonstrate experience
- You convert ideas and concepts into a purchase order

Creativity plays an important role in all aspects of the connectivity process. It not only leads us to approach customers and clients with a freshness of thinking; it also pushes us to develop tactics that differentiate us from our competitors.

Creativity is all about changing the way we think. It can also be about how we can use problem solving to benefit the people that we want to work with. In later sections of the book we'll share some simple creative tactics that will help position you closer to the prospect in order to beat the competition.

Building and maintaining relationships is the key to long-term, sustainable business development. Underpinning successful relationships is the ability to deliver your promises on time. It should be one of your key tasks to build those relationships and achieve a synergistic relationship with targets and customers.

This can only be achieved by obtaining an understanding of what your client or customer is trying to achieve, then marshalling you and your company's resources to delivering true value within a given budget.

THE FIRE INSIDE YOU

Principle 3 – momentum

It is a fact that confidence speaks very loudly to potential customers and partners. If you feel bad about yourself then that *also* will quickly become obvious.

An ability to feel good, express confidence and deliver a motivated performance completes the picture.

On the flipside, a lack of focus, direction and motivation are often a by-product of what can often be a very difficult job. The role of business development is probably one of the most visible areas of any business where both success and failure are clear for all to see.

But we've all been there; missing opportunities preys heavily on the mind of anyone actively involved in the business acquisition arena. It's those business development professionals who possess a true streak of resilience that are the ones that reap the benefits in the long term.

How we manage our affairs outside the job also impacts significantly on performance. Our family, finances, and health all have a direct impact on how effective we are.

Inner and outer confidence are drivers of momentum

building, and ensuring that a high drive is maintained when things get tough is a vitally important lesson for every business development professional to learn.

Each of us has a unique personal brand that is imprinted on a prospective customer's mind. That brand must be worked on and modified to suit the characteristics and personality of the buyer we are dealing with.

It is the degree of comfort that we have with our personal brand that makes each one of us unique. It is what's called 'just being yourself'. Our natural talent, energy, and drive flow freely from just being ourselves – it's only when we try to put on an act or try to be something or someone that we are not, that things go wrong.

We'll go on to see how we can find this natural state of balance and ultimately achieve a state of sustained peak performance. Not only will this help you professionally, it can also create greater freedom of thinking and attitude in all elements of your life.

CHAPTER 3

How Are *You* Performing?

Our 'Pitch Perfect' equation is your starting point from which you can begin to understand how you're shaping up as you strive to achieve the peak performance you'll need to succeed. Our aim is to excel in each of the three components.

Continuous improvement is relevant to everyone; outstanding performers are always aiming to perfect their game. The guiding principles of 'Pitch Perfect' effectively translate into a set of core characteristics and behaviours that help secure this positive circle. It's these principles that we'll be seeking to develop and drive forward throughout this book.

> We are what we repeatedly do. Excellence, then, is not an act, but a habit.
> *Aristotle*

THE GUIDING PRINCIPLES FOR 'PITCH PERFECT'

- **Functional Mastery** The possession of subject, organizational, marketing and industry matter expertise that conveys credibility – the basis of consultative selling
- **Customer Connectivity** A highly creative approach to finding, winning and keeping business
- **Momentum** A skill that helps us think and act as a winner, highly motivated and assured of making a personal impact

BUSINESS DEVELOPERS – SPOTTING THEIR GENERIC APPROACHES

Over the years, we've come across all sorts of different business developers with their own unique blend of skills. What's also been clear to us, however, is that it's relatively easy to categorize business developers, each with their own generic approaches.

In our view, there are four core categories of business developer:

The Rough Diamond

These are the fast talking business developers who possess low levels of functional mastery skills. Their inability to understand the needs of their prospects or customers leaves them typically "winging" their way in their relationships. Rough Diamonds tend to:

- Exphibit high levels of energy
- Lack specific evidence of successes
- Communicate rapidly
- Use jargon without always appearing to understand what it means
- Ignore prospect/customer wants and needs
- Use pressure tactics
- Lack team focus

The Crashing Bore

Crashing Bores possess high degrees of functional mastery skills but their interpersonal skills and use of selling methodologies tends to be low. Such individuals:

- Are highly technical but only really understand their own market offer
- Miss buying signals because they are so keen to talk only about their offer
- Overwhelm prospects and customers with jargon (the difference here being that they actually understand what they're talking about!)
- They often fail to excite

- Cannot adapt to different types of buyer personalities
- Poor interpersonal skills

The Steady Eddie

Steady Eddies are often the backbone of many organizations and ensure a steady stream of business from both new prospects and existing clients. Typically they are:

- Well versed in their offer and have a good command of functional mastery skills
- Convey confidence that their services will be competently delivered
- Their interpersonal skills require development
- May have difficulty working with certain types of decision makers
- Recognize the importance of a team approach to selling
- Offer reliably modest levels of business development success
- Are usually mildly receptive to innovation, but ultimately like to do it the way they have always done it

The Winner

The Winner exhibits a high degree of competency and entrepreneurial flair and is the true star of a successful organization.

What marks these people out? In our experience, these individuals possess most or all of these attributes:

- Have a clear sense of purpose and self direction–leadership
- Excel in interpersonal relationships and are charismatic in their approach. They have an ability to empathize at all levels
- Usually demonstrate high degrees of functional mastery. In instances where this is lacking they use a team-based approach

- They provide specific examples of success
- They utilize leading-edge problem solving tools and have an open mind to new tools and techniques and apply them
- They can create and innovate to apply new ways of tackling customer challenges
- They practise what they preach
- They have high moral standards and personal values
- They can interpret the needs of clients and translate them into no nonsense solutions
- They are excellent time managers
- They are highly motivated and resilient to challenges
- Think of themselves as their customer's peer
- They sell from the heart and are passionate about their job

DEVELOPING THE RIGHT STUFF

The Appendix provides a self-assessment for you to check how well you are performing in each of the three guiding principles that are encompassed within Pitch Perfect. This assessment is not definitive; it does, however, cover the main attributes and characteristics you'll need to maximize the likelihood of success.

Complete the assessment honestly and total your scores. Once you've done this you can multiply your total to work out your percentage. You'll then be able to mark each of your totals for functional mastery, customer connectivity and momentum on this radar diagram:

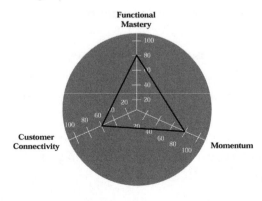

BALANCING THE PRINCIPLES

You're looking to achieve an even balance across all of the three areas. If you are scoring less than 40% in any of the three areas, then search for the reasons why:

- **In Functional Mastery** Look at your knowledge of your products or services. Are you fully competent in the key elements of what you are offering?
- **In Customer Connectivity** Are you practising creative ways of doing things? Are you stuck in doing it the way you have always done it?
- **In Momentum** Are you losing direction in your life? Do you feel fit and healthy? Are you thinking like a winner?

We think it's a good plan to repeat this self-test every three months, and your goal should be to score over 80% on each of three checks – and clearly, what you're after is to achieve a "full circle" – balanced excellence in each of the three areas. Our section on Staying Focused later in the book will help you develop a clear improvement plan that focuses on those vital areas that need addressing.

. . . AND FINALLY, GET IT DOWN ON PAPER

If you're not sure where your strengths and weaknesses really lie, there's extensive evidence to suggest that writing down your own perception of how you see your good and not so good attributes helps to focus and crystallize improvement requirements.

So – here's your opportunity to do so. If you wish, you might copy this into a notebook so that you can build your points more easily.

Today's Date:

What Am I Good At?	What Do I Need To Focus On?
1.	1.
2.	2.
3.	3.
4.	4.
5.	5.

Make a note in your diary to re-visit this checklist once a month. You'll then be able to look far more objectively at this initial self-analysis, and you might also want to amend your thoughts as you develop your strengths and work to weed out your weaker areas.

PITCH PERFECT: THE THREE PRINCIPLES

SECTION TWO

PITCH-PERFECT:
THE THREE
PRINCIPLES

CHAPTER 4

Functional Mastery

If you really want to sell well to prospects and existing customers, one of the most important attributes you'll need to possess is credibility.

Credibility breeds confidence. It assures prospects that the offer your organization will provide is likely to meet and exceed the promises that you make. It also makes it far more certain that existing customers will turn to you to secure additional goods and services and maximize your long-term profitability.

> Functional mastery is the process of bringing together the knowledge of the company, the market, competition and products and services to the benefit of solving customer problems. It is the foundation of credibility and trust.

THE BIG PICTURE – ARE YOU IN THE KNOW?

Excellence in functional mastery is achieved when you understand and can manipulate the 'big picture' of the climate in which you are operating.

An intimate understanding of this big picture establishes your credibility. As business developers we *have* to be passionate about the company we represent and the products or services we sell. This passion manifests itself in enthusiasm and will send the right signals to decision makers.

> You can't beat passion. It manifests in enthusiasm and action!

Matched to our passion for our organization and its products or services is a holistic knowledge of the industry of which we're part. Knowledge is the most valued commodity of all. Today, we sell

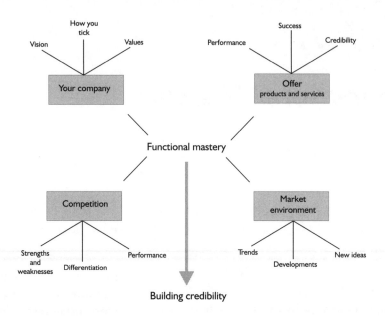

solutions; in doing so, we add value to our customer's business. In order to do this we must understand all the facets of the arena in which we operate.

KNOW YOUR COMPANY

The company we represent is the umbrella under which all promises are made. Virtually any prospect or customer will want validation that they are dealing with an organization that is "decent, honest and true." In making any presentation, it is paramount that we fully promote our organization with pride and that any offer is made against the backdrop of a fully supportive and integrated team of people who are committed to service delivery. The key messages to communicate are:

Your organizational CV

Prospective customers will always feel more comfortable with you and your organization if they are brought up to speed on its history and credentials. The growth phases and key landmarks of your company's development are important to clients and potential customers. A proven track record of successes is a good basis on which to communicate a credible business. This track record can be demonstrated through the articulation of core achievements, including successful new products launched, customers secured, international development, strategic alliances and so on. Regardless of whether you're a founder, a shareholder or simply an employee, it's vital that you understand the key milestones of your business and its leading personalities.

Financial standing

Prospects and customers want to deal with financially sound businesses. You should therefore aim to demonstrate a positive financial picture in terms of financial health and rectitude, your investment history and strategy and your goals for future development.

Customers

It almost goes without saying, but prospects are far more likely to buy from you if the peers and competitors that they know and respect are seen to be clients of yours.

References, then, from your clients speak volumes both to potential and existing customers. If you have a list of blue chip clients let your prospects know. It essentially sends the message that if 'they' engage your services then you must be doing something right.

Capacity and resources

Every customer – whether new or long standing – wants peace of mind that you can deliver what you say you can, when you said you could, to the level of quality they believe that they have bought.

Often there is a tendency to overstretch resources and commit to deadlines you cannot meet, simply to win an order. This is a temptation that many suppliers find difficult to resist, but unless you're extremely lucky, it is usually a recipe for disaster.

In the long run, it is those businesses that can clearly show their clients that they have the ability and the necessary resources to meet their needs that succeed.

In short, passing the capacity and resources test is a vital part of the confidence building exercise needed to establish trust.

Facilities

The vast majority of clients want to be associated with success; the facilities that you possess are a clear manifestation of your success, and are therefore important weapons that you can call on. A state of the art office, a major piece of machinery, leading edge instrumentation, and information technology – make sure that prospects and clients understand what you possess, why you invested in these areas, and what benefits accrue to your customers through you possessing them.

Shout loud about your good news

You can keep up your corporate propaganda in the market and to your prospect and customer audiences by shouting loud about your successes, whether they are in recruitment, products, ideas, customer wins or new premises. This is a vitally important process. It attracts new prospects; it reassures existing customers; it engenders healthy respect amongst your suppliers and industry peers; it encourages applications from high-quality candidates when you are recruiting.

Quality standard accreditation

Securing quality standard accreditation in your industry is a clear message to clients that time, effort and investment has been directed to improving the way that you do business. As a business development professional, this is an area of specialism that might not fall under your direct remit, but don't let this put you off. Find out who's job this is; make sure that the organization is prioritizing this as a key corporate objective; assist in securing and maintaining accreditation; and, when you've achieved this standard, make sure that you communicate this to your prospects and customers alike.

Awards

Winning business awards reflects your ability and success as an organization. Successful companies and business developers use such accolades to demonstrate to prospects and customers that a policy of winning is embedded within your organizational culture.

People

People make organizations tick. If, through clear leadership, an environment has been created that instils a motivated and vibrant workforce, then this will be tangible to potential customers and clients. Although modesty usually forbids, here's what one of *our* clients said when they us recently:

> *"There is a buzz about Strategem – what a fantastic place this must be to work"*

KNOW YOUR OFFER – PRODUCTS AND SERVICES

How well do you know your products and services? Can you talk with a high degree of authority about how they perform and what they can achieve?

This seems like a statement of the obvious but all too often we have seen business developers, and this includes many senior managers, turning up to clients and potential clients without a real purpose or message about how their products or services might enhance their target's
well being. *No* Purpose! *No* Result!

We will go on to see in subsequent
chapters how getting under the skin of clients' needs is largely down to preparing your case.

Selling on the hoof is unprofessional and fosters a lack of

trust and a misunderstanding of the client's needs; try to wing it and your credibility will undoubtedly melt away.

Information dissemination is part of any meeting with potential clients. You must remember that when you are selling, barriers will exist, particularly if it is a new customer that knows little about you or your products.

You should ask yourself the question – why should this person see me? You should be thinking that your product or service has a clear benefit for your prospective client. Be clear what this could be prior to any meeting.

Such situations require you to demonstrate your presence by a clear understanding of:

- Your product or service, backed up by real examples
- The right questions to ask
- The need to possess the materials, such as a presentation, brochure or working example/prototype that will reinforce your credibility

By maximizing your functional mastery skills, some of the barriers to success can be removed prior to a first point of contact. Establishing credibility can be achieved by preparing materials, case studies and information of direct relevance to the client.

KNOW YOUR CUSTOMER'S MARKET ENVIRONMENT

It is often expected that as professional business developers we have a clear understanding of the industry and business environment that we operate in. There are many factors that impinge on our customers' wellbeing and prosperity, including industry trends, global issues, the health of the financial markets and environment legislation. A professional business developer should possess a sound appreciation of relevant issues and how they might impact on their clients' or customers' ability to purchase.

After all, if these factors affect our customer's decision to buy they could also create challenges in the future. Many of these global issues are out of our control, but if we are conscious of these driving factors then it puts us in a better position to respond and to solve problems.

Stay one step ahead of your customer by understanding their market environment. You can shape their thinking.

Moreover, understanding the climate in which our customers operate can help us create new solutions by helping them shape some of their future buying decisions. This is a key element within the consultative sell, which we'll return to in a later section of this book.

Demonstrating our knowledge and understanding of an industry or market is a good way of showing our interest and concern with our current customers; it is also an effective way of keeping in touch with potential customers.

Keeping in touch does not necessarily have to be a costly exercise but in today's increasingly crowded market we have to differentiate ourselves from the competition and keep our customer informed. We must budget and provide an effective resource for such actions. It is a powerful way not only of demonstrating functional mastery but also showing a clear

---

Top tips for conveying your understanding of the commercial climate

1. Send cuttings from press or industry journals
2. Put an industry update on your website
3. Issue monthly email or white mail bulletins focusing on what's new
4. Make impromptu phone calls to customers; "did you see that article in…"
5. Hold regular customer days
6. Do a monthly Reuters search and send details

commitment to customers that we are in fact working in partnership to the mutual benefit of both parties.

KNOW YOUR COMPETITION

In today's environment business is becoming increasingly competitive. Me too strategies are outdated and their long-term sustainability is questionable.

Gio Benedetti, one of Scotland's most formidable entrepreneurs talks about the need to differentiate ourselves from competition. As professional business developers we must prioritize differentiation. This means that as an integral element of functional mastery we need to intimately understand the workings of what other suppliers are offering:

- Their product/service portfolio
- Strengths and weaknesses of their offering
- Breadth of their product range
- Level of service

One of our golden rules of business development is that you should avoid the temptation to bad mouth your competition. It is vital that they are professionally respected but your offering should be clearly differentiated and support materials and examples should be readily available to underline the points you make. By talking authoritatively about the competition's offering you will demonstrate an understanding of the market place, how it works, and how yours is the superior option for the buyer.

In this arena of understanding the competition we can draw some simple lessons from football. What have many successful team managers got in common? They spend hours watching the tactics of their competitors both on tape and at live games. They ensure that they become experts on their tactics, how the ball is played and what position key players adopt. In

---

Knowing your competition – learning lessons from the football "pitch"

Bill Shankley, one of the legendary soccer managers from the 1970s, used a form of competitor analysis to help Liverpool become one of the world's most feared teams. It is rumoured that he sent two club officials to watch and closely study the tactics and strategies of the teams his team were due to play – both UK and in European. His men monitored each second of the game with precision and detail they took copious notes of : team configuration, defending and attacking strategies, passes, free kick tactics and indeed detailed strengthens and weakness assessments were made of the players. This information give Bill Shankley a clear picture as to how his team should respond, their counter tactics and what his team needed to do in order gain competitive advantage. All in all these tactics contributed to Liverpool's success.

Apply these Pitch tactics to your business – it will help you stay one step ahead of the game!!

---

short they focus on quantifying the strengths and weaknesses of the opposition.

They can then develop their tactics and organize their gameplan according to how they want to approach the game. In business our competition can be viewed at exhibitions, through websites and from brochures. Once we have identified their strategies, it helps us to position our products and services and make a clear differentiated offer.

WHAT MAKES YOU DIFFERENT?

How many times have you been in a meeting when you have been asked "well, what makes *you* different?"

At Strategem we have spent hours deliberating what makes our consultancy different. It is a natural follow-on from

> **Know what makes the difference?**
>
> The head of Procurement at a multinational automotive company was giving a presentation to suppliers. He said that his first question to any supplier is "What is different about what you have to offer?" He stated that 7 times out of 10 suppliers will go into a long drawn out presentation that misses the mark. It usually starts with a long list of clients and details of what is in the toolkit. Pretty dam boring really. What he really wants to hear is an introduction like " the new air filter developed can improve engine efficiency by 50% and its technically proven" His concluding remark being that the 21st-century sales person must be a consultant, problem solver and a relationship manager.

understanding what your competitors do. In our case we believe that our company possesses the ability to *'translate strategy into action and deliver tangible results for our clients'*. This means we show a direct link between our client's investment in us and the results – the pay back – that our intervention has created.

We sincerely believe in our uniqueness and we strive to deliver it with passion. Being different attracts attention. It's also the factor that gives you a competitive edge.

There are some simple techniques that you can apply to evaluate what makes you different.

- You should always ask your customers for feedback
- It's a straightforward process to review your competitors' websites
- It's also pretty easy to obtain their brochures
- Ask your customers about how they read the market
- Talk to your suppliers – this will 'round out' how you interpret the market

- How about talking to your competitors – potentially through the forum of your trade association
- Take a close look at your competitors' PR and communications strategy
- Take the trouble to identify those employees who have recently joined you – their view of the outside world will be fresher than yours

When you have done this, map what you think:

- Your competitors are good and bad at
- What your competitors can deliver that you can't
- What you can deliver that they can't

What you're looking for as you go through this process is a clear picture of your unique selling points and what makes your organization different.

Be sure to believe in what makes you different

Armed with this information you'll be in a much stronger place to talk authoritatively about your positioning and how you will bring added value to your client's operations.

Showing you are different

Here's a good example of differentiation. A client of ours in the construction products market conducted an analysis of their sector and quickly realized that architects and building contractors were rapidly moving towards a "just in time" system of demand, where product orders were placed very late in the process to minimize damage and cut inventory costs. They audited their production capability, and realized that by reorganizing some elements within their manufacturing, they could move to a "next day delivery or your order is free" offer. Predictably, sales boomed – and so did their profits.

There are some important messages within this model. Our client took the process of differentiation very seriously. They realized that they would have to change the way they did things to create a real customer-driven difference. They marshalled the entire forces of their business to make change within their production process happen; and they also geared their investment in capacity to cope with the upswing in demand that their new differentiation created.

Get this far, and you'll deserve all the success you achieve!

SELLING THE ORGANIZATIONAL SPIRIT

Your organizational spirit is the atmosphere within which your company operates. It is what makes your business live and breathe. It comes from:

- Strong, well focused leadership
- A clear understanding of the purpose of why people come to work
- A passion for products and services
- The differentiators that makes the company unique
- The values that govern the behaviour and practices of the people within the organization
- The feel-good factor that envelops a team approach to business

We'll hold our hands up at this point and say that identifying, creating, developing and sustaining an inspired organizational spirit is perhaps beyond the scope and remit of Pitch Perfect. What we *will* say is that your job of the business developer is made far easier if you truly believe in the purpose, values and vision of the organization that you represent.

When the beliefs of the business are truly captured and articulated to a prospective client, then a natural passion is released, and it's one of the most powerful selling tools imaginable. If this energy is clearly visible then the wheels of doing business are sufficiently oiled to pave the way for relationship development and making a sale – as long as you *truly* believe that your products or services can make a difference to their operations.

As business developers we need to truly understand the corporate priorities, values, strategic thinking and heritage of our organization as it is these factors that will shape the way in which our people operate and develop. Prospects and customers want to hear about the growth and evolution of business as long as they are backed up with real examples of how they are manifested in action or tangible benefits.

Selling your values
Here are our own company values. This is how we make them real to customers.

- **Customer Focus** – we have a customer charter that guarantees 100% satisfaction.
- **Continuous Learning** – individuals are encouraged to develop their specific skills in a given area. They then produce 'thought leadership papers' and make them available to customers.
- **Commitment** – we bend over backwards and always meet deadlines and promises we make.
- **Speed** – enquiries, emails and phone calls are returned within 24 hours.
- **Teamwork** – a diverse range of skills are made visible on all contracts.
- **Enjoyment** – That would be a secret!!!

Never underestimate how critical the above are!
This area needs some degree of practice to articulate effectively, but it's one that you should endeavour to develop.

MAKING IT REAL

Functional mastery is the process of intimately understanding how your product or service can add value. This means that you know without doubt what can be done or what can't be done within your offer.

Sounds good; sounds obvious. The hard bit comes when you have to make this difference real. Only then will it come alive and the prospective client is in the best possible position to evaluate your proposition.

- Maybe your software *can* add efficiencies to a customer's accounting processes – this is critically important so *must* be quantified
- The office furniture you are selling provides a better working environment. You must bring to life and make real what you mean by "a better working environment"

Words are fine but how do you make your products, services and ideas come to life?

Especially if you're selling services, creating a tangible dimension to what you have to offer is particularly difficult. In the consultative selling process it's important that you can find mechanisms and ways of crystallizing your ideas into something that the prospective customer can relate to. Here are some of the ways you can make your story real and enhance your skills through functional mastery:

- **Case Studies** Write up past histories of what you or your company have done. Take pictures and send them to your customers. Build up your own portfolio.
- **Testimonials** Letters of satisfaction, news articles, and press references that detail success on projects, new products, new markets and people. It's what others have said about you and your company that is important!

- **Models**   Mock up your ideas in the form of a model or prototype. You can talk for hours about a new concept idea but it's only when a prospect can see it and feel it that they're in the best possible position to appreciate your approach.
- **Animate, Illustrate**   Draw pictures, take photographs or use mind maps to demonstrate your ideas. Use video presentations to show your product or service in action.

FUNCTIONAL MASTERY – THE MASTERCLASS

You don't have to work in business to be a master of your function.

Lance Armstrong has won the most gruelling prize in sport – the Tour de France – five years in a row. Sir Steve Redgrave has won gold in five successive Olympic Games. Others, from the arts, politics and religion, have achieved similar iconic status. Quite rightly, people like these Functional Masters capture a massive following and become role models to people in all works of life.

What, as business developers, can we learn from them? What is it about them that makes them special?

Successful individuals from these different walks of life have one thing in common: they have mastered their subject and

---

A functional master class

- Functional Masters continuously learn and read
- They have a clear purpose and vision
- They take time to reflect and think
- The more they practice the better they get
- They continually search for new ways of doing things
- They're passionate about their interest or course
- They communicate their message with a high degree of clarity

---

through this they achieve excellence and are recognized as role models. These people are passionate about their cause. Whilst most of us will never achieve the dizzy heights of stardom, we have our own stage in the customer's office or boardroom. Here is our chance to excel and make an impact and apply some methodologies and thinking from the world's functional masters.

There are key messages from the masters that we can use to our advantage. Try this and see the effect it has on your understanding and approach:

- Identify someone who you admire as a functional master
- Write down the qualities you think they possess that make them masters of their field
- Think about how they communicate to their audience
- Write these points down!
- Put them into action!

FINDING A MATE

In a recent survey of highly successful people, in nearly all instances respondents laid a large amount of emphasis on their reliance either on a role model or coach, or possibly both. There is a subtle difference between the two. A role model is effectively someone who we can learn from. A coach is someone who has an active intervention in our personal and professional development. In some instances the two could be the same person.

The use of role models has become an important tool in the development of functional mastery. Tony Buzan, creator of Mind Mapping, refers to the use of his mastermind group. This is effectively a group of people that have excelled in their own field and who are there to act as a source of inspiration. The Mastermind Group technique has parallel applications in the third momentum element of Pitch Perfect.

In functional mastery we should use role models or

coaches from our industry or from within our own companies. They are primarily those individuals who are more experienced or who have a particular skill in a given area. We must not underestimate how powerful such individuals can be to help us learn and to continuously improve our knowledge.

Many business development professionals swear by the process of 'buddies' or 'buddying up'. Junior members of staff spend a significant amount of time with more senior personnel, both with prospects and with clients, and within the office back at base. This process builds on the theory that people learn most effectively through observation and through guided insight. A buddy system allows us to:

- Pick up knowledge and expertise
- See how more experienced people put across messages
- Discuss case histories of projects and experience, and understand why things went well
- Pick up anecdotes that make real other customers' buying experiences

Although it's true that irrespective of where we are in an organization we can all learn from each other, it's also the case that the more senior we become the more difficult it is to find a 'role model' or coach from within. Senior people within a team often have to look elsewhere for a 'role model', perhaps from a related business or sector. Wherever it is from we should not

---

Key messages
- Take note of how colleagues communicate key corporate messages
- Make a note of anecdotes they use
- Ask if you can accompany colleagues to meetings
- Identify people from your industry that you can relate to

lose sight of the fact that if someone else has succeeded they are more than happy (usually!) to share their insights and expertise with others.

WHERE DOES THIS LEAD?

Functional mastery is the building block of the business development process. It is what provides the "aura" of credibility in terms of:

- Your company
- Yourself
- Your product /service offer

. . . and credibility is the basis upon which all successful contracts and orders are won. It is also the basis from which you can begin to establish a synergistic relationship with your customers. If they believe in you, your company and how your product /service can bring them value then it provides the basis of a long and happy association. More specifically . . .

You build confidence with your customer

The confidence factor is vital. It is like the trust we place in a doctor's advice. Very rarely do we question it. We often take their word for granted. We, as business developers, must draw the parallels with this thinking so that we can effectively diagnose a customer's needs then apply an appropriate remedy. That remedy is what we have to offer. If we don't have the appropriate solution or we feel the problem is out of our sphere of expertise there is everything to be gained by referring to a subject expert within your business.

Whilst most of us don't like to admit we don't know the answer, credibility is built with customers when you can provide a sensible alternative that is:

- Real
- Believable

- Beneficial
- Cost-effective

This is the process of leaving the door open and the basis of the 'team sell' that we will go on to talk about.

You build trust

What's the first thing many of us think when someone says 'trust me'? It's often "I don't trust them", isn't it!

Trust is earned. It is centres on following up the promises you make with actions. Trust is built up over time and does not have an immediate impact. In functional mastery, trust is initiated by proving real examples of past successes and testimonials from satisfied customers. We will go on to see how you can make real the statements made to customers and potential customers.

You avoid the spiv factor

None of us want to be viewed as a spiv but unfortunately that's how sales professionals are initially viewed in many instances. Remember you are there to help, offer advice and demonstrate how an investment in your product or service will create a valuable benefit for your customer. By mastering your offer you will create a positive business environment where both parties enjoy an output that is mutually beneficial.

A consultative sell is approached strategically

Selling complex systems and solutions is all about problem solving. Business development involves getting under the skin of your prospective customer's problems and putting forward options that clearly demonstrate a return. This is often a challenge, but ensuring that you have drawn a parallel between an investment and the expected return maximizes your chances of success.

In our own selling efforts at Strategem we make a major feature of what tangible outputs a client will receive from buying our services. To avoid the derogatory comments that management consultants often receive, we have differentiated ourselves by telling customers exactly how an investment in our services translates into financial benefits. This could be in terms of new business, cost savings, or increased productivity. It focuses the customer's mind and is an excellent route towards expert positioning.

The benefits you'll derive from this approach to business development are enormous. It can be your key to the door and the element that differentiates you from the competition. It is also the underpinning factor to the consultative selling process:

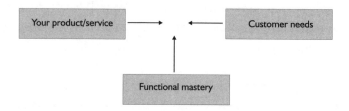

Marrying what you have to offer with a customer's needs depends on you possessing a thorough knowledge of your offer, and how real benefits will be accrued by your prospective customer if they buy into your company's products/services. You will gain respect and be viewed as an integral element of your customer's team.

GETTING THE BALANCE RIGHT

Displaying a guru-like knowledge of your product, service and market is vital in business development as it helps to sell ideas and keep one step ahead of your customer, but when you're in discussions with clients and customers you also need to know when it's appropriate to shut up!

Everyone can recall an occasion when we've seen someone that is so involved with their product or service that they just offload their expertise and overwhelm their audience.

Learn to read the signals – drooping eyelids are often a clear indication that saturation point has been reached!

Achieving this balance will result in:

- Interest from the customer
- Good rapport between buyer and supplier
- Barriers being lowered
- The start of a relationship

Just make a mental note next time you are discussing your product or service with customers. Are you saying too much? Recognize when it is time to stop – bring in the real examples to make the discussions interesting.

YOU BECOME THE EXPERT

Getting a grip of functional mastery is an important component of establishing a superior personal brand where you become an acknowledged industry expert. But how do you build this overriding sense of expertise? Well, some ways you can do it are shown in the following box.

Becoming the expert – some tips

1. A great way of telling the world you are the expert is by writing articles for leading industry journals and send PDF versions to your customers – append them to pitches
2. Make yourself known to the industry's key journals, periodicals and editorial staff. (If you or your company has paid for advertising tell them that you want editorial space)
3. Keep your CV up to date and add in new skills and expertise
4. Get yourself on the 'speaker circuit' and give presentations at events, conferences and other gatherings of the industry's great and the good

---

5.   Make yourself visible on the organizations' websites as a leading expert in your field of expertise
6.   Make yourself the voice of the industry and attend industry meetings and forums
7.   Put together 'thought leadership' papers together, i.e. your view on the industry and send them as booklets to your customers

Whilst this process may seem to be extremely laborious the benefits to be derived from establishing a 'guru' status in the market is enormous as we have said in other parts of the book – The Customer Comes To You!

UNDERSTANDING FUNCTIONAL MASTERY – A CHECKLIST

- Functional mastery brings together company, product, competitor and market knowledge – get briefed thoroughly
- Keep abreast of market and technology developments. This will ensure you stay one step ahead of the competition
- Knowing competitors inside out help you to establish a differentiated offer
- Be clear on what makes you different
- The intangible 'organizational spirit' provides comfort to customers. Use it. If you have not got it work on it!
- Use real examples to demonstrate your knowledge and expertise
- You learn from the masters – chose your master, act like them
- Find a mentor, coach or mate – someone you can learn from
- Build a 'guru' status – be visible in the market place as the font of knowledge

We Want You!
"The Guru"

CHAPTER 5

Customer Connectivity

How long does a sale take to achieve? In many ways, this is almost an impossible question to answer. Clearly, if the purpose of Pitch Perfect is to focus on ways in which we can share our understanding and experience of the consultative selling process, then the development of a sale – from prospect analysis and prioritization to the first cheque in the bank – will involve many different elements.

Some sales can take a number of years to come to fruition, and these more complex cycles will be characterized by the sheer scale of the commitment, investment, energy, patience, persistence and often anguish, which is frequently how real life happens for companies with high value products/services.

While sales processes that are measured in years may be the exception to the rule, it is not uncommon for some accounts to take six to twelve months to open and gain an order. This is because selling is changing; customers want a high degree of technical knowledge and input from their suppliers and indeed they also require high levels of intervention and partnership in order to develop solutions and solve problems.

> The overriding objective is to become a valued resource to the customer rather than someone who sells.
> *Robin Fielder, Sales and Management Guru*

Functional mastery gives us the tools, confidence and ability to engage in those discussions that help us to meet these challenges. Customer connectivity, however, is about identifying, exploring, winning and keeping the relationships with those people that really matter to us in business. Seeding, nurturing and maintaining these relationships are key, because they provide a business with long-term sustainability, ultimately providing the stakeholders of an organization with a return on their hard earned efforts and investments.

But remember it is also getting much more competitive and harder to win business. Just look at what's happening:

The squeeze is on so sharpen your pencil

It has been reported that companies are reducing there suppliers by a third as compared to 10 years ago. Look at the facts: Ford has reduced the number of suppliers from 52,000 to an astonishing 5,000. IBM disposed of 40 advertising agencies now they have one. Boeing will over the coming years reduce the number of its suppliers from 30,000 to 9,000.

ENTERPRISE STRATEGY – SETTING THE DIRECTION

'Pitch Perfect' brings together the personal development and practical tools needed to secure customers and achieve success. However a primary requirement for effective deployment is that an enterprise strategy and vision is established. This means that:

Getting the best from Pitch Perfect

There is a market for the products and services being offered	✓
Ambitious growth targets are in place	✓
Resources are available to fulfil contracts to high levels of satisfaction	✓
A business has a clear sense of purpose and direction	✓

'Pitch Perfect' is the driving force that creates organizational success. Any business worth its salt has a balanced base of customers; one major customer does not govern its livelihood; it has a broad customer base of retained clients and deploys sensible budgets that provide fuel in the customer generation tank. Remember, successful businesses:

- Grow their sales and profitably
- Diversify their customer base
- Win new customers
- Successfully launch new products and services

'Pitch Perfect' provides the route map to making it happen.

CONNECTIVITY SPECTRUM

Before any deal can be done with a new customer, you'll undoubtedly embark on a journey with them.

This journey will comprise a number of stages, which we've termed connectivity points, and these mark the path between receiving an enquiry to getting a purchase order. These connectivity points will assume different positions within different markets; some will be straightforward, others will be tortuous and demanding. They all, however, lie on a Connectivity Spectrum:

Connectivity spectrum

Let's have a look at each point on the connectivity spectrum in more detail.

Enquiry

Enquiries are generated by a variety of means, and are the end product of your organization's marketing programme. Here, techniques encompassing advertising, public relations, telemarketing, sales promotion and focused mailing will all play a role in generating new leads. This is allied to, but different from word of mouth recommendations, or the leveraging of existing contacts, as these essentially stem from an established awareness of the abilities of your organization. We will go on to see how in 'Golden Rules' reaching new customers is all about making an offer that they can only say 'yes' to.

Pre-qualification

In many industries, you may need to satisfy technical, legislative, or informal sector-driven requirements that dictate that you need to clear a pre-qualification hurdle as a prerequisite to further advancement. This, obviously, could well be a time consuming process that involves putting forward credentials in preparation for a project or delivery of goods / services. Customer vetting is applied and a rigorous screening of resources and capability is commonplace amongst many blue chip or public sector organizations. This does not guarantee a contract; it merely means that you are an approved supplier. More work to be done!

First date

This is the first and most important time that you will have to impress a new prospect. While it's true that the potential customer may have already established an emotional link with you and your business – through previewed literature and visits to your business's website – there is still no substitute for making first impressions count. Key issues to consider here are that you have the 'props' to make your impression and impact. Remember in functional mastery we spoke about demonstrating how you solve customers' problems. Have you done your preparation? Do you know where they are coming from? Have you 'sat in their shoes' to think about how you can make their life easier? Are you ready to focus, ask the right questions, listen to their answers, second-guess and interpret their needs?

Tender lists

Getting on a tender or pitch list can often be a product of your initial meeting. It may have been what was needed to move closer to the customer – an opportunity to pitch for a piece of work

Pitch preparation

This is the time to galvanize your resources and develop your solution to meet the prospects needs that will answer all the questions. Who will work on the pitch? Who are your big ideas people? Who's going to do the backroom research? Are your admin team ready to turn your vision into a tangible pitch? Who will actually stand up and talk? Who will write the submission? When will you review? When will you rehearse? Get the answers to these questions right and you'll be well on your way to preparing a winning pitch.

It's worth, however at this stage raising a word of caution. If you are invited to pitch for a project out of the blue then, good for you . . . *but* – you may just want to temper your excitement with a little retrospection. Why has a pitch dropped in your lap without you being aware that this particular organization was even in the market for your kind of offer? Are you being lined up to compete against far better positioned opponents? Is there *really* a deal in the pipeline, or are the prospects merely trawling the market for new ideas? If you've any doubt of the veracity of the opportunity, do some digging around with contacts or old colleagues who're working for your competitors. You owe it to yourself and your company not to pile into a pitch process without first ensuring that a deal will be in the offing, because after all, you don't want to waste time and effort when a contract has already been earmarked for someone else.

Presentation

In some industries, a written submission may be the only chance you have of securing a contract. In others, the hard copy proposal will go hand in hand with a personal presentation. Some markets, of course, rely almost completely on a "beauty parade" where you have been short listed to pitch. This is where you are on centre stage to persuade the prospect that you and your organization possess not only the credentials, proposition and imagination, but also the right personal chemistry to make the deal work. A presentation of this kind is your opportunity to capture the audience with a lucid vision of what life will be like if your two businesses work together. This is where the hard work of the pitch preparation stage will come to fruition.

Contract negotiation

Negotiating the contract. It's here that the new relationship is frequently put under its first serious test. Both parties bear the responsibility for delivering a win–win result from this process; if the balance falls too heavily in either side's favour, resentments can quickly surface that can throw months – or years – of hard work away. As a supplier, your key challenge is to show to your new customer that you fully understand and that you can articulate back to them their expectations, and that you genuinely believe you can meet and exceed these expectations within the financial framework imposed on the relationship.

Continuum

After the deal has been done, it's up to you to maintain the client relationship as effectively as you do from Day One. This means that you must possess strong and reliable retention processes, as it's no use securing new business wins if existing clients are falling through 'the hole in the bucket' at the other end.

UNDERSTANDING THE FIND, WIN, KEEP MODEL

Whichever way you look at sales and business development, there are three core elements of the cycle to be considered, as illustrated in the figure on the bext page.

It's worth flagging up an important point that concerns not only you in your business development role, but your company from a wider perspective. What is of primary importance in this cycle for any business is that there is a healthy balance between finding and securing new prospects and ensuring sufficient time, effort and resources are given to the retention and development of existing customers.

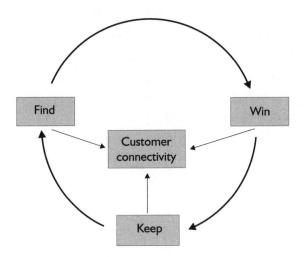

As most of us know, existing customers drive turnover and profitability, and it is far easier and more cost-effective to retain and develop them than it is to find new ones. Every business should possess two processes; one that is responsible for identifying and securing new customers, and one that is responsible for existing customer retention and development.

While business developers must ensure that the finding stages of customer connectivity require . . .

- Sound market intelligence
- Innovative ways of identifying customers
- Effective marketing
- Effective lead generating mechanisms
- Creative presentations that demonstrate a desire to win
- Differentiated marketing strategy
- Sales collateral

. . . It's also your responsibility – if not necessarily (though often actually!) part of your brief to ensure that your organization is similarly resourced and focused on retention, encompassing

- Open, clear and balanced contract processes
- Lucid relationship methodologies

- Measurable review opportunities
- Diaried client/programme update meetings
- Internal reviews to check on delivery quality
- Processes that enable you to surprise and delight the client by going beyond the call of duty

CHAPTER 6

Momentum

What do all successful business developers have in common? They all have a desire to win.

Winning, inevitably, also means that they possess the ability to cope with setbacks, continue to think positive and have the resolve to drive towards the finish line.

These are core competencies that we must all aspire to hold. Coming second in business development might be a learning experience but it doesn't pay the bills, so the attitude to win must be embedded both within the individual and at an organizational level. We mentioned earlier that selling is the most visible function and process within any corporation, so coming runner-up is not an option.

Momentum building is all about taking ideas, thoughts, customer contacts, leads and opportunities and driving them towards a purchase order and a cheque that can be banked. All too often we get caught up with detailed strategy, plans and visions but ultimately you have to get out there, wear out the shoe leather and keep banging on those doors. Momentum is the fuel in the tank that drives strategy into action:

Momentum

Strategy ⸻⟶ Action

Just do it. Everyone is familiar with Nike's exhortation to sports people. It's a powerful line, because it cuts to the chase (literally!). Momentum is all about recognizing that inner feeling and drive, the 'inspired you' that can conquer the world.

Frank Dick, the former coach of the Great Britain Olympic team, who is now a professional management coach, talks about mountain people and valley people. The mountain people constantly strive for the next goal and win, the valley people sit within a den of security and are quite comfortable in their blanket of no risk. Ask yourself – which one are you?

He who hesitates is a damned fool.
Mae West

Momentum in physics is defined as mass multiplied by velocity. Your mass is your functional mastery and knowledge. Your velocity is your get up and go; your speed of reaction.

You need to get busy, get positive, get focused, and target your efforts in one direction.

The inspired, highly tuned, peak performer with high degrees of momentum:

- Gets out of bed in the morning and is clear about what they are going to do
- Stays focused during the day and has everything under control
- Gets excited about new prospects and challenges
- They are clear about what they want and how they get it
- Their own personal brand equates to win and success
- They are just as alert at the end of the day as when the day started
- They do what they say
- In the face of adversity, they continue to manage

Tick all these boxes, and you've got momentum. Your drive, your positive work ethic and personal imprint will impact on both your colleagues and customers. Peak performers combine momentum with functional mastery and customer connectivity skills that culminate in success.

Books, CDs and tapes really can help energize, motivate and drive us. Go into your local bookstore and have a look. Try them and use them regularly either in the car, at home or whenever. Constant reference to such materials will help to create a climate conducive to making it happen and success!!!

The key is to build up the steam train feeling and crash through the barriers in life that stop us from getting to the final destination. Here are the golden rules of building momentum.

THINKING THE RIGHT WAY

A common trait of many of today's successful business developers is their ability to think in a way that is conducive to success. Conversely, some people seem obsessed with seeing the barriers that block their path.

Barrier Thinking might comprise:

- Seeing hurdles
- Always focusing on reasons why not
- Problems exist before they present themselves
- The pursuit of new ideas are always a waste of time

Jack Black, the motivational expert, talks about how such thinking programmes the brain, to produce negative thinking that in extreme cases leads to total inertia. Jack advises his clients to state 'Delete that programme' when such negative thoughts reveal themselves. With constant practice and application the grip of such negative comments can be released but it takes lots of practice and self-control – Just try it. Thinking in a more 'can do' way creates an enormous opportunity for the business developer. Sometimes ignorance is bliss as it avoids baggage often associated with old ways of doing things.

Thinking a positive outcome is the route to success. "A State of Mind" sums it up perfectly.

So the first lesson in momentum building is to think in the right way, view customer opportunities, new projects, new business opportunities and pitch prospects as challenges and

A State of Mind

If you think you are beaten, your are
If you think you dare not, you don't
If you'd like to win,
But you think you can't
It's almost a cinch you won't
If you think you'll lose, you've lost,
For out of the world you find
Success begins with a fellow's will
It's all in the state of mind

mountains that can be conquered. In other words: **as you think, so shall you become.**

This is probably one of the most important messages for a business developer proactively seeking to secure new orders and contracts. Believe in the fact that all things are possible then your behaviour will slowly but surely align itself towards doing all the right things you need to do to make it happen. Limiting beliefs inhibit high performance. It is vital that we view opportunities as endless and think in such a way that our behaviour mirrors this thinking.

I believe the mind is the most powerful weapon : we either use it to achieve great wonders, or allow it to destroy us. I have for many years chosen the former.
Merlene Ottey, World Champion sprinter for the past 20 years

IT'S NOT JUST THE JOB

How we do at work – whether well, so-so or poorly – is not always down to the job and our professional scope. Your performance can often be related to factors outside the work environment. In many instances, personal factors can play a part too. Think about the following factors:

- **Finances** – Are you worried by bad debts or a big mortgage? Are you paying for something you can't afford? Have you stretched yourself too far?
- **Relationships** – Are relationships suffering as a result of your work? Do you have issues with a teenage child or with your partner?
- **Socializing** – Do you have interests outside of the work environment? What takes the pressure off your work?

- **Your Job** – Do you have a clear sense of purpose or direction? Do you feel under valued? Are you making the maximum contribution given the skills you have?
- **Fitness** – How fit and well are you? Do you take regular exercise? How often do you take time for energizing your body? How's the drinking – and the eating?
- **Learning and development** – Do you have all the skills? Are you a functional master? Do you feel comfortable in the areas in which you are trying to sell? Or do you feel your skills are outdated?
- **Outlook** – Is everything you do a hassle? Do you see the positive or negative aspects of what you do? How do you think about the future? Good or bad?

The important points to stress here are that if any one of the above issues is out of balance or causing a problem then they can impact negatively on our ability to perform well. They can slow us down and momentum can rapidly turn into inertia. It's important that you continue to review these issues so that you can take action or seek help and advice to overcome them. The work–life balance wheel can help us understand what life issues need addressing.

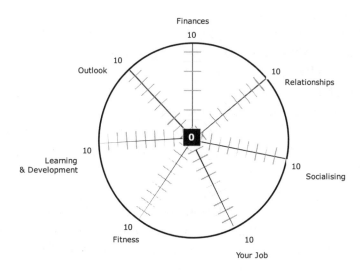

Score yourself on the wheel and ask yourself: Am I balanced? Are there factors at home or in my personal life that are impacting on my momentum? Clearly identify what they are and write them down:

Factors affecting your momentum
1.
2.
3.
4.
5.

Once you have identified what those issues are, then you are in a better position to address them and take appropriate action to solve them. It won't be easy to overcome some of these areas, but the biggest breakthrough that you will make is when you recognize that a problem or issue exists. Only at this point can you start to look at your life as a whole and decide what steps to take.

Personal vision
Ask yourself: What are you doing all this for?

This isn't an easy question to answer. Yes, you might be in it to make money. You might also be in it for the sense of achievement – the buzz.

But for many business development professionals, it's also about something else. They possess a real vision of what they want to achieve, and how they see the business world around them. They harness this vision to a series of values to form a true bedrock that creates their sense of purpose.

Where there is no vision, the people perish.
Proverbs 29:18

Ask yourself: Have you ever had the feeling of wandering around in the wilderness and have no clear sense of direction or purpose?

If you answer yes to this question, perhaps it's time for you to work on your own personal vision. Without a clear vision of your ultimate destination, a lack of direction could push you into an aimless rut and cut your own momentum.

The truth is, of course, that you're not going to conjure up a vision over a cup of coffee. It's an evolutionary process that crystallizes over months or even years. Look at what Goethe had to say on this.

In other words, once you have established a clarity of purpose, an immediate force or series of actions will begin to affect your life, behaviour and things you do on a daily basis. A new direction emerges that will result in meeting new people, embracing new ideas and reaching for new possibilities that will put you on course to realizing the vision.

> The moment one definitely commits oneself, then providence moves too. All sorts of things occur to help that would not otherwise have occurred. A whole stream of events; all manner of unforeseen incidents and meetings and material assistance which no man could have dreamt will come his way. Whatever you can do, or dream you can, begin it! Boldness has genius, magic and power in it. Begin it now.
>
> *Goethe*

Hints and tips on creating a personal vision
1. Start off and check your work–life balance sheet
2. Mind map and thunderbolt what you would like to achieve
3. Think about your mastermind group – what have they done and what can you learn
4. Write down your goals

Research conducted at Yale University has shown that success in business life is down to establishment of clear goals and targets. What is more important about this research is that those high flyers actually wrote their goals down on a piece of paper. The message is clear – write down *your* goals in a personal notebook or on a notepad and review them regularly. You don't have to reinvent the wheel when tried and trusted techniques are easily available.

PERSONAL VALUES

There are unwritten laws on ways in which we should behave and operate with customers (and indeed colleagues, friends and relations). In the business development role we have discussed in detail the role of trust and relationship building. Personal values play a vital role in this arena. Most of us will have experienced over the years, both in a buying or selling situation, the following feelings:

> *'Would never do business with him and his company again'*
> *'Will never trust her again'*
> *'That was a pretty shabby way of being treated'*

Displaying a positive, humanitarian work ethic and *modus operandi* is, in our view, a vital component within the make up of a successful business development professional. Our experience has shown that the most successful business entrepreneurs actually display the right kind of human qualities needed to build relationships and partnerships.

Values are the principles upon which we run our lives and make decisions. If you want someone to spend money on your products and services then they have to trust you – genuinely. We firmly believe that business developers must operate to high moral standards of behaviour that comprise truthfulness, honesty, fairness and pride if they want to sustain their success. Yes, you might make a buck faster by bending or breaking the rules, but it's actually a harder game to play year in, year out, and there are very few people who can live with themselves in the long term by operating in this way. If your values are positive they will do both yourself and others good. Regular practice of sound moral value will always win in the end, these will become habits that customers respect and

Thoughts manifest as the word;
The word manifests as the deed
The deed develops into habit;
And habit hardens into character
So watch the thought and its way with care
And let it spring from love
Born out of concern for all being.
Buddha

value. Over time your market will recognize who the good and bad operators are.

Here are some of the most commonly mentioned positive values of successful business developers.

Truth	Understanding	Trust	Simplicity
Patience	Integrity	Humour	Tolerance
Honesty	Gratitude	Equality	Responsibility
Co-operation	Courage/bravery	Persistence	Speed

What we'd now like you to do is to choose seven character-istics from this set of positive behaviours. Which seven do you think you display? Are there seven here that you aspire to por-tray?

Once you've chosen, we'd like you to focus on them and make them your Seven Guiding Values. They'll now act as the base for your moral and ethical business development and sell-ing approach.

Choose Your Seven Guiding Values Carefully – They're Going To Be With You Forever

PERSONAL BRANDING

Pepsi's got a brand. Levi's got a brand. Tesco's got a brand. Have *you* got a brand?

Branding has for many years been the domain of the large corporation under the control of the advertising gurus. How-ever, in business development, personal branding should also be playing an important role to help differentiate you from the competition.

As we have discussed, business development is about sell-ing yourself, your company and the products/services – and probably in that order too.

People buy brands, and this concept is very easily transferable to an individual. Since we've discussed how the intangible relationship is so important in successfully securing complex, high-value sales, getting your personal brand right is very important for:

- Differentiation
- Giving customers the confidence in you as a person
- Building your reputation in the market place
- Being viewed as a person who the market should be doing business with

If your personal brand is synonymous with quality, delivery and functional mastery, you – and, therefore, the organization you represent – will be sought out, and guess what? Price will become less of an issue, enabling you to command a deserved premium in the market. People will pay for quality.

Here's how it works:

Establishing a superior personal brand

The three components of the personal brand comprise:

- **Functional Mastery** – an ability to solve problems and provide solutions to customer challenges. Such individuals are characterized as industry experts with knowledge that is highly sought after. Typically they would present at conferences on their area of expertise and have a proven track record within industry.

- **Social Mastery** – an ability to engage with people. They are articulate and present well and are generally very well liked. They attend industry functions often, are exceptionally well known in the industry or market place. They are also closely associated with other industry winners.
- **Spiritual Mastery** – individuals that exhibit strong values. Their chosen Seven Guiding Values are synonymous with an excellent reputation and they are known for keeping their word.

Developing and maintaining high levels of personal branding also leads to lowering the cost of sales and indeed is an effective way of attracting business to you.

Here's the wish list that you should strive to achieve as you develop your own brand:

- You've an excellent reputation
- You're well known in the industry/market
- You've a reputation for high quality service
- You've supplied some of the best companies
- You're regularly featured in the trade press

Get this right, and you will almost certainly attract customers without having to chase too hard.

It's also worth mentioning the importance of marketing yourself. As you grow in confidence that your own personal brand is on track, you

> There will be time to prepare a face to meet the faces that you meet.
> *T.S. Eliot*

should also consider how to market this into your sector and how to make yourself remembered by others; what's your unique selling point, and how are you going to project this?

A man with a difference

One of our clients has built a highly profitable and successful engineering business in recent years. He's known in his industry as one of the best engineers with an unequalled knowledge of solving problems. Not only is he well liked by all his customers and peers, Chris has a reputation for service, quality delivery and keeping his promise. So far, so conventional.

This is where the fun begins. Our man is over six feet tall. He's built like the proverbial brick outhouse. He shaves his hair so close you could mistake him for a skinhead. He's the only engineer we've ever met that wears two earrings. To look at him he looks like a bouncer at the local nightclub.

So what's the point?

This guy is such a one-off that people want to associate with him and want to give him the business. He has made himself stand out in the memories of his customers. This is a great example of the 'Restorff Effect' or the 'Outstanding' or 'Memorable Principle'. The principle states that we remember those things, people, places that we associate in our brains as *outstandingly different*.

Building your personal brand
1. Define your functional, social and spiritual elements
2. Be clear on what you stand for – your passion for the products and services you represent
3. Be consistent in the messages you project
4. How does the Restorff Effect apply to you?
5. Great personal brands are known for the company they keep – associate yourself with winners!

SELF-LEADERSHIP

Your own personal vision is in your hands – only you can make it happen. You're the CEO of Your Own Life Ltd!

All too often, we blame others for our own shortcomings, when in fact, we should probably look closer to home.

> What lies behind us and what lies before us are tiny matters compared to what lieswithin us.
>
> *Oliver Wendell Holmes*

Self-leadership centres on being in charge of your own life and the way in which you go about your daily activities to achieve the end result. Self-leadership is the process of taking ownership of this process. In directing your efforts ensure that:

- **You are ready for takeoff** – Your vision and values will govern how you manage your life, so you need to make sure that the activities you engage in are aligned to your vision. Be clear on and ready for the challenges that await you and view competition as an opportunity to learn and improve.
- **Work with the best** – Achieving success means that we have to surround ourselves with people that often have better skills than ourselves. Find them and work with them. They will help take us to our final destination. Associate with optimistic people not with negative ones, the former will act as a psychological support in times of trouble.
- **We are all the same** – In the spirit of comradeship it is vital that we view everyone as equals. The best business developers in the world view themselves on the same level as their customers – not inferior, not superior.
- **Get the best from people** – The networks you establish, your peers and immediate bosses – understand their strengths and weaknesses. Build and use the strengths of the surrounding people to help you overcome the obstacles you face.

- **Extending comfort zones** – New situations, new opportunities, and breakthrough thinking mean that we have to stretch our capabilities. In those situations be brave and courageous and go for it. Calculate the risks first but don't let fear be a barrier – push yourself to the limits.
- **Be truthful with yourself** – Understand and be clear on where you are in relation to the destination. St Benedict said: leadership is about knowing when to be a loving father and when to be a taskmaster. To us this means praise yourself when its going well but equally when things are coming off the rails drive yourself hard to get back on track.

STAYING ENERGIZED

How many times have you faced some of these challenges?

Long days	Lost business
Early mornings	Competitor tactics
Extensive travel	Bad run of sales
Big customer demands	No leads

Staying energized in these situations is not always an easy task to perform. If we let a run of bad luck linger too long in our thinking we become depressed. Our activity levels fall, our momentum drops, we lose our effectiveness and inertia sets in. Sometimes, the harder we try to pull ourselves out of this dip in form, the worse it seems to become.

What do we do if long hours, travel and customer demands make us feel like we're approaching burn out?

Winners re-energize. They've built up a clear idea of when to work hard and when to back off. They have gained a better perspective of how they react to stress and what is likely to trigger it within them. Like professional athletes, they recognize that relaxation time is as important to their performance as hard work in balancing their productivity. They have worked hard and possess a relentless sense of self-motivation. They're then able to:

- Overcome obstacles
- Face challenges creatively
- Discourage project hijackers
- Avoid derailment through others

We've seen a number of common traits exhibited by those that have an ability to stay self motivated and energized. Here are seven of them:

> I know of no more encouraging fact than the unquestionable ability of man to elevate his life by conscious endeavour.
> *Henry David Thoreau*

1. Maintain a belief that every obstacle contains an opportunity
If you don't share the philosophy that there is good in everything then you will quickly become downhearted. When faced with challenges, you should train your eye to see the opportunity. Faced with a rapidly declining market for a product that represented 85% of his company's turnover, a client of ours took this cue to develop new products. The company went on to triple its turnover and double its workforce.

2. Be your own best friend
If you don't believe in yourself then nobody will. The use of self-affirmations should play a very important role in your life. Keep telling yourself you are a proactive thinker, an extra miler, a winner and a great business developer.

3. Follow your vision
We talked about the importance of creating your own personal vision. Maintain this vision as a positive reality and follow your dream. Self-motivation is heightened greatly when we engage in tasks that truly energize, captivate and lead toward fulfilment of the dream.

4. Persistence, patience and perseverance

Ask once, ask twice and then ask again. It's important to keep asking, chipping away and waiting. As the old saying goes 'nothing in life comes easy'. Children seem to have mastered this technique. How many times have you seen parents giving into a child's demands just to find some peace?

5. Visualize yourself being successful

"Those that can see the invisible can do the impossible" is a statement that appeared on the business card of a motivational consultancy firm we met in California. When the mind visualizes the future and there is a deep belief in a person's will that it is possible then a powerful force helps to create that future.

6. When you fall off your bike get back on

> Obstacles are those frightful things you see when you take your eyes off your goal.
> *Henry Ford*

The business development journey is filled with unexpected pitfalls, disappointment and setbacks. The key for continuing self-motivation is to get back up when you fall. Abraham Lincoln's business went bankrupt twice, he lost eight elections and suffered numerous breakdowns but he still became president of the United States.

7. Forgive yourself

Being honest with yourself is vital, but constantly telling yourself that you got it wrong does nothing but de-motivate. View failure as feedback on how you can improve and what needs to be improved. This learning experience you go through when you get it wrong is merely part of the cycle of continuous improvement. One of the best ways to learn is to experience how not to do it! Next time round you will try a different approach.

> Failure is only the opportunity to begin again more intelligently.
> *Henry Ford*

MAINTAINING SELF-ESTEEM AND CONFIDENCE

Self-esteem is slightly different to self-confidence; it's the trust that we place in ourselves. However the two are inextricably linked and one cannot work without the other. If we don't trust ourselves, then we have no chance with the customer. The task is to build high levels of self-esteem that translates into the kind of well-directed confidence that captivates prospects and customers.

Self-esteem is not everything its just that there's nothing without it.
Gloria Steinem

People with high self-esteem have a strong sense of self-confidence. They like themselves, they can manage their internal state and they have a clear sense of purpose. Those with low self-esteem are not able to recognize the good results they keep achieving, cannot hear praise, and feel inadequate to fulfil a task they are more than able to take on.

In contrast, people with true self-esteem exhibit the behaviours of quiet confidence, they accept compliments they know they are worthy of; they're often humble, and they're interested in other people and their achievements.

In the business development and selling arena a high degree of self-worth is vital if we are to build momentum. We must believe in ourselves and our ability to win. Suffering set-

---

Maintaining High Levels Of Self-Esteem

1. Practise the Treat In The Same Way technique. In all situations behave in the way you would expect to be treated. The more you practise this the more natural it will become

2. Always talk about what has worked and been successful. This helps to focus on the positive

3. Always keep your biggest successes in your mind. Keep reliving these successes

4. Accept yourself and be happy that you are you!

backs can seriously change self-esteem, however there are some simple tools that we can apply to ensure self-esteem is maintained at peak level.

SPEED – ACT FAST

How speedy are you?

The spirit of time shall teach me speed.
Shakespeare

Get good at being speedy, and you'll turn jobs round quickly and avoid procrastination. Being speedy is easy. You can:

- Pick up the phone instead of writing a lengthy email
- Tell someone what has gone on instead of writing a report
- Turn pitches round quickly
- Be available at weekends or whenever someone needs to talk to you

As Rene Carayol says, if you are going to fail, fail fast and then move on. Speed is a value that is practised by many successful people; all too often we can think about things for too long. Trust your gut instincts and use intuition as a tool to make decisions. Judgement plays a very important role in our ability

---

Creating speed – tips

1. Return calls quickly.
2. Open your email and act – don't keep going back to it
3. Reduce the time to go through the think, plan, do, decision cycle.
4. Do not always strive for perfection. 90% right is often good enough
5. Find every short cut possible to hit the target. This means delegation to peer groups, boss and team
6. Do it now, don't drag the job out

to shorten the lead times to making a decision. Most of the decisions we make in business follow the patter of:

Think → Plan → Do → Review

We should endeavour to reduce the time within which we make decisions. In this way we get more done in a shorter timeframe. As the world gets speedier, if we don't act fast our competitors will, so no procrastination – Just Do It!

PLUGGING THE GAP

We can't always have the full complement of skills needed to fulfil a task. In business development we can rapidly sink into

---

Knowing your stuff and asking the team

The MD of a medium-sized company that sells advanced metal machining services to the aerospace industry was becoming increasingly concerned with the ineffectiveness of their sales engineer, Steve. This well-turned-out, mid-30's sales guy was well presented and an articulate communicator head-hunted from a multinational engineering company. Steve was responding to enquiries but the level of quotations were beginning to take a steep fall. We were asked to undertake a customer survey to identify the problems. Whilst the apparent reason was increased pressure on price it became very apparent that the issues were much deeper rooted. The design staff had very little confidence in Steve's knowledge of metal forming techniques. His inability to talk in depth about the technical aspects led to him losing credibility fast. Consequently competition was mopping up the business.

Corrective action was needed. Steve was excellent at getting in through the door, but could not cut the mustard when it came to engineering talk. Product training was of paramount importance, as was closer working with his own company's

---

engineering team. Once the small talk was over and initial introductions and capabilities had been presented, more technical
support was brought in through his technical and engineering
staff colleagues. Quotations rose as a result and conversions into
sales were amazing. Steve's history with a multinational provided
more extensive back and support. In his new role the resources
were not as freely available. He felt uneasy asking for help in his
new environment. The new team approach led to renewed
success. By accompanying technical staff to meetings over a six
month period, it led to increased confidence levels and greater
credibility with customers. His learning also strengthened his
functional mastery.

inertia by not having all the skills in place to win. Plugging the
gap is achieved firstly through recognizing the resources that are
needed to complete a deal. Secondly we have to use our leadership skills to mobilize our resources.

Plugging the gap
1.   Look at every opportunity in terms of the Pitch Perfect
     equation. Which bits are you missing? Define the gap and
     assess what you need
2.   Broaden your network of associates and contacts such that
     you can call upon them when needed
3.   Talk openly to your network about what you are up to.
     They may see gaps that they can fill
4.   Don't be too proud if someone you know can do a job
     better and it takes you to your destination – ask for help
5.   Be clear on colleagues' capability in other departments and
     divisions
6.   Keep your networks alive

All too often we steer away from business opportunities because we feel that we don't have the complement of skills to satisfy need. By building our personal networks through your company and through partnerships and alliances we are able to take on much more. These networks allow us to find more customers, broaden the offer to customers and provide better quality. In business development we should be seen as a Mr Fix-It, someone with an ability to find a man who can.

GET RID OF THE OLD WAYS

If we're working in the business development environment, we have to be feeding through a constant source of new possibilities.

A major barrier to sales inactivity or inertia is doing things the way they have always been done.

> **It's time to think differently**
> A global survey of 178 executives looking at the sales effectiveness was conducted by Accenture and the Economist Intelligence Unit. It identified as one of the top performance issues that – an amazing 58% of the respondents felt that their sales teams were *"Stuck in the Past"*.

Do the same thing, and it shouldn't be any surprise if we get the same results – a constant theme throughout this book. This stuck record habit inhibits our thinking and our ability to proactively seek out solutions to finding, winning and keeping customers.

The primary message here is 'get rid of the old stuff' which means:

- Manage your stress – it totally inhibits creativity, creates a block and you will go nowhere with new ideas. Take regular exercise and get yourself down to the pub!

- Do it different – instead of going down the same path of doing things, break up the routine and approach your daily tasks in a different way. Even something as simple as driving into work a different way or buying a different newspaper can be enough to trigger a fresh approach
- You don't want to do it like that, do it like this – Rubbish! Don't let your own opinions, views and attitudes impinge on your colleagues' approaches to business development. Sit back and observe occasionally, see what the outputs are. Don't let your own values and beliefs always take the lead!! You might start to learn.
- Don't be afraid – lots of business developers and sales people are afraid of trying out new ideas for fear of being laughed at. Well, the fact is that in business development we have to sometimes be 'off the wall'. Overcoming fear is often what is needed to make the mark. We'll go on to see how bravery and courage play a pivotal role in selling – *'Feel The Fear'* – *Susan Jeffers*
- Know when to stop beating yourself up – selling is an arena where setbacks are inevitable. Self criticism is an effective tool in moderation – but apply it too much and you'll start to impact on the way you approach the challenge in front of you
- Don't let the b******s grind you down!

BUILDING MOMENTUM – A CHECKLIST

- Momentum gathers pace, inertia holds you back
- Think the right way – you become what you think
- Check your work–life balance wheel – are there external factors impacting on your ability to build momentum
- Have an Away Day with yourself to create your personal vision and be clear about what you want to achieve in life

- Write down what your personal vision and associated goals. Use the road map concept to plot where you are and where you want to be
- Select your Seven Guiding Values to build a positive reputation
- Define your personal brand and establish what makes you different
- Develop your self leadership skills as this will guide you to achieving your personal vision and break through challenges
- Practice the seven rules of self motivation
- Raise your trust in yourself to improve your self-esteem and self-confidence
- Don't mess about – act fast – Just Do It!
- Recognize your shortcomings and plug the gap. Do whatever is needed in terms of working with others in order to get the right result
- Break up your routines and just develop a new life pattern for a week. Don't get stuck in a 'rut'

PITCH PERFECT: FINDING, WINNING AND KEEPING CUSTOMERS

CHAPTER 7

Finding the Opportunities

So, we've established a clear picture of the value of functional mastery to the business development professional. We've taken a look at the customer connectivity spectrum and seen the degree to which each stage of the process is integrated. We've also viewed the components that are vital to developing personal momentum. It's now time to take a closer look at finding, winning, then keeping new business.

First, let's review the key principles of finding new opportunities.

GETTING IT ALL MAPPED OUT

How do *you* look at the shape of your market?

The following box ("The market landscape") is what three business development decision makers said about how they saw the opportunities that existed in their own particular sector. Put yourself into each of their shoes for just a moment, and perhaps it's quite easy to see how they look at the world. Each product offer; each market place; the climate, levels of competition, investment, history and future potential of each sector all come together to build a unique composition and provide our interviewees with a series of cues that influence the decisions they make about finding new business.

It's clear that the new business director of the metallic inks business must approach 90 target customers across the world in a different way to the techniques adopted by a UK-only building product supplier faced with 1,200 architects who are buying and

---

The Market Landscape

"Our business sells metallic ink pigments into the international paints and dyes markets. There are around 90 target customers for our products around the world, and I'd guess I know —or know of – them all by their first name".

"My company makes highly specified composite aluminium and wood window solutions for the commercial new build market in the UK. I'd estimate that there are around 1,200 specifiers in the UK that make or break our business".

"I'm responsible for selling a market leading lager; I've around 30,000 potential customers in the on trade, and a handful of buyers in the retail market – but around 20 million consumers in the domestic market, and millions more around the world".

---

specifying products for their clients. Neither of their experience and priorities will be similar to the way in which a brewery business builder works with the buying teams of the leading supermarket chains, their major pub business clients, and, ultimately, the general public.

Each road map to success in these three examples will be completely different. What *will* be the same with these companies lies in two areas. *Firstly*, they will possess a map that scopes out their market in an analytical way, so that it encompasses where potential business lies, what the routes to market will look like, and what the issues and challenges to success might be.

Secondly, each business will maintain and develop this plan to ensure that it is continually evolving and staying in touch with changes. Interestingly enough, the commercial landscape facing our three companies here has, to a greater or lesser extent, changed beyond all recognition in the last few years, with legislation, shifts in demand and taste production costs and so on – meaning that yesterday's business development solutions are no longer appropriate in today's market or for tomorrow's likely direction.

Have you mapped out the shape of your market? Do you know how many key decision makers there are, where they're likely to be, and what the significant issues are?

RECOGNIZING THE ICEBERG OUT THERE

A common feature for many of us is that we can often quite clearly 'see' the big opportunities for our products and services. However, these targets are the ones that are most difficult to hit because both domestic and internationally based competitors think in the same way.

Moreover, while we may clearly understand where the 'big ticket' opportunities exists we often forget that the nuggets may be elsewhere – usually beneath the surface!

In other words, the larger, visible, "glamour" opportunities might only account for around a fifth of the business that *truly* is out there. It's a question of looking under the surface. This has enormous implications because unearthing the opportunities means that we have to:

- Be proactive and understand the marketplace
- Research the marketplace thoroughly via a broad sweep of techniques
- Use a variety of approaches to identify opportunities
- Investigate and network to understand and prioritize opportunities

- Be proactive and highly motivated to ensure we are covering the ground effectively
- Be willing to be persistent and resilient – it's a long-term process

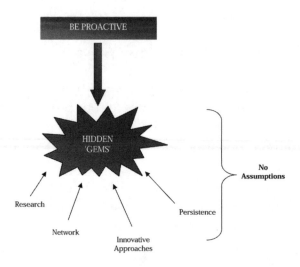

Business development professionals will be able to encompass both the high value low volume "glamour accounts" within the same mapping exercise as the lower value, higher volume opportunities. In doing so, they will build in checks that remind them *not* to make assumptions about the levels of potential or extent of opportunity.

So, is it possible to research and analyse every prospect, where all potential opportunities are sifted, graded and prioritized? The real answer is – no.

SELLING FROM 'GUT FEEL'

Many of the best business development professionals overlay their intellectual analysis of their market with an intuitive feel that points them to some of the most profitable seams to mine.

Where does these hunches – this gut feel – come from? Intuition springs from experience, a clear understanding of market dynamics, industry structure, what has worked in the past, what has not, comments from suppliers, customers and competitors – this all helps fuel the feeling we get about a commercial situation where hard evidence is difficult to find.

When we get these hunches about an opportunity we should not ignore them because our 'inner mechanisms' are effectively telling us that there is a need to explore.

> A hunch is creativity trying to tell you something.
> *Frank Capra*

Here's a scenario that could be applied to many commercial sectors

The name of a potential customer had been mentioned to the business development director of a professional services agency. The director in question was led to believe that an opportunity to meet this possible target could be arranged.

The only problem was that the target would view such a get-together as "just a chat", with little to presume that there would be a business benefit.

The director made further outline investigations and established that a meeting could be arranged, but it wasn't likely that she could spend more than an hour with him. It would involve a 300-mile trip to make the 9.00am appointment.

One voice in the director's head said "forget it, you need the time in the office", but this was overwhelmed by another saying "you have *got* to go".

The loudest voice won the day. The meeting went ahead. The director and the target hit it off, and the agency was later invited to pitch for a prestigious contract – provided it could deliver plans within a two-day deadline. The agency succeeded, and the relationship, which now stretches over a ten-year period runs into millions of pounds of turnover.

Why did this director go with the "yes" voice in his head, when he knew there was no tangible business on the table?

He realized that all buyers are ultimately looking for solutions. Even if his target had no immediate needs, sooner or later she would consider his agency to solve a problem for her. He also understood her position in his commercial map – she was a key contact and a signpost to a vitally important portion of his market. He saw this as an opportunity that might not come round again – even if all that came of it was "a chat", if he made a positive impression he knew that she might become an informal ambassador for his business. Conversely, if he said no, sure, he would have saved some money, a day in the office and a lie-in on a Monday morning, but she might have mentally crossed him off her shopping list for good.

So, you can see that actually, although hunches can be intuitive, they're also the subconscious application of a series of deductions that, although difficult occasionally to justify to your organization's financial director, actually make a lot of business sense when the decision is analysed.

As with many of the messages within this book it's about balancing the analytical with the human. The key here is to *think*

Key lessons for gut feel selling
1. Approach opportunities with 'fresh' thinking – remove old baggage
2. Don't make assumptions
3. Listen to what your inner voice is saying
4. Does it feel right (ask yourself honestly – no pet project)
5. If it does feel right go for it and gather more information
6. Don't be proud to say you were wrong if you are
7. If you are right – let everyone know!!!
8. Know when to say enough is enough

about your approach – so you can always say that you've considered all options!

FINDING CUSTOMERS

Customers are the lifeblood of any business. They are the basis upon which all corporate ambitions are built.

We've now looked at how a combination of the analytical and intuitive represents the most effective combination of mapping out and prioritizing prospect acquisition.

Unless you're our metallic ink pigment supplier who can name his 90 possible targets, it's likely that you're going to need something more rigorous to finding your customers. Research is a key competency for any successful business developer and being able to access a variety of sources to help pinpoint new customers is a necessity for filling up the prospect pipeline. Here are some of the most common routes to identification of new prospects, bearing in mind they generally emerge from two primary sources:

Where will the business come from?

Leveraging existing contacts

One of the fastest routes to winning more business comes through the links and networks that we have through our existing contact base. Have you considered whether:

- A customer you are supplying can provide contacts into subsidiary organizations or related businesses?
- To ask if your customer can provide names of other people that may have an interest in what you are supplying?
- There are overseas subsidiaries that could be tackled

through the work you're undertaking in the domestic market?

- There are well-recognized experts in your sectors that have a clear and well-informed understanding of your market, who could point you towards new opportunities? Frequently, editors of industry publications, or industry consultants – many of who are semi-retired and have been on the scene for a number of years – often have their ear to the ground, and know who might be looking for new suppliers. It's often worth giving them a call, getting to know them, or buying them a drink – it could be an excellent investment!

Never assume that your existing contacts would have told you where other business opportunities might exist, because while it may be a prime objective for you it may not be for them! There are six simple words that work wonders for the business developer:

Please can I ask your advice?

It is our experience that eight times out of ten an influencer or decision maker, if asked for their advice, will be more than happy or willing to assist, advise and if possible signpost to new possibilities. So why is this so?

- You are making a person feel important and recognized
- You are expressing value in their judgement and experience
- Most people (usually) want to help others

This question should not solely be linked to existing customers; it can be used in any context where knowledge or information is required. Try it and see how far it takes you. We have found this approach to be instrumental in opening new doors and seeking out new contracts. It is a very powerful tool, as long as you keep your "informant" up to speed and that any progress you make is acknowledged and recognized.

Try it and see for yourself – it really works!

Making market knowledge really count

Remember the last time you took a walk down your local shopping centre? There's a reasonable chance that you might have been stopped by someone with a clipboard and asked if you'd be kind enough to answer some questions about your views on this product or that service.

This didn't take place for any other reason than market research. For years, businesses have realized that if they were to fully understand their sector, they needed to continually keep in touch with the people who really counted – their current, potential and lapsed customers.

True, most of the businesses are likely to be consumer-oriented organizations, but there motives and actions can teach those of us in consultative business development some important lessons about the value of understanding our market space.

> Knowledge makes a god of me.
> *John Keats*

Advertising, public relations, and so on can be defined as outbound initiatives. These, essentially, are where a business indulges in a programme of activity that is designed, in various ways, to raise the profile of itself and its offer, and where the business can act on these responses and include the best leads within its business development strategy.

This is another occasion where we'll need to hold our hands up and acknowledge that a debate about the merits – or otherwise – of these techniques is beyond the remit of Pitch Perfect. What's important here is that you recognize these opportunities and commit some time to further improving your knowledge so that you're better able to make informed decisions as to their value to your organization.

It's also worth remembering that you don't necessarily

need guess work, luck, or big marketing budgets to scope your market and identify likely customers. Frequently, purchasers out there are just as eager to let you know they're in the market as you're keen to tell them that you can meet their needs. Why should this be?

If you stop to think for a moment, the answers are pretty obvious. The vast majority of businesses that you're probably targeting are seeking to buy in products or services to meet their own needs, add to their own wealth, and improve their own profitability.

Yes, they want best value, best price and best solution. But they also want to buy efficiently from suppliers that they believe can best do the job for them. Procurement professionals won't want to keep the fact that they're in the market a secret – it's not in their interests to do so. In fact, the more rapidly and clearly they can brief the pool of likely suppliers of their requirements, the better.

Once you digest this point, it's easier to understand why businesses and organizations publicize details of forthcoming tenders and opportunities to pitch. Get to know the way in which your market sectors do this. It's increasingly likely to be through specialist websites. If you're looking for further help why not contact the leading trade magazine in your industry, or speak to your trade association.

CHOOSE YOUR CUSTOMERS

Whilst it may seem arrogant, you should try to be selective about the customers you decide to do business with.

Why? Well, choose the wrong customers and you might find that your problems have only just begun.

How about these hassles to start with:

- Lengthy payment periods or even worse not getting paid at all

- Constant irritations and petty questioning over how you conduct your business
- Ongoing pressure to reduce prices
- Disruptions to other customers
- Low margin, poor added value

The best advice, if you're to avoid dealing with this breed of customer, is to differentiate your offer and to create added value without compromising margins.

From a strategic viewpoint, the business development function is your organization's driving force for new offers, operational improvements and quality. It is the ears and eyes in the market place. Wherever possible the business developer should endeavour to identify new product opportunities, emerging gaps in the market place, spot and counteract competitor strategies and create an ongoing feedback loop into the broader strategic and operational functions of your business.

Good customers are the lifeblood of successful businesses. Bad ones can be damaging, so care must be taken when choosing those partners we want to do business with.

We must view our customers in terms of how will they enable us to achieve sustained profitable growth with opportunities to learn, grow and introduce new thinking. We must select our customers.

But how, you might ask, should I discriminate between a good and bad customer? Here's an easy way of checking whether *you* think they're worth working with – the 4F's screening tool. Make sure that you can answer 'yes' to each of the following:

Fame

Will your targeted customer add value to the profile of your business and provide you with added credibility in the market place? Will the fact that they are reference points help you secure more business and position you as a leader? Will other potential customers find it attractive that you are supplying a reputable and prestigious organization?

Fortune

Are you going to make money or will it be a financial nightmare servicing this account? Will you get paid on time? What are the payment terms? The sale is not complete until the final bill has been paid. All too often we grab at business and later on down the line we wish we hadn't bothered. I'm sure most of you will have experienced instances where you shouldn't have bothered with an account because financially it was not worth it and it was just too difficult to secure an acceptable level of financial reward in return for the service provided. The key message is – don't take in dirty washing or grab at business – you may regret it!

Whilst we have said this, there are accounts that in the early days may not provide the financial return, however, securing the business has longer-term implications on winning other customers that has strategic value in its own right.

Fun

It's always a pleasure doing business with someone or with an organization that creates fun. Life is too short to be mixed up with hassle and awkward people. Whilst the latter are a feature of our jobs, we must learn when to recognize when individuals or organizations will make our life a misery and business difficult to conduct. We can view fun on the following scale:

Customer fun index

At Point A of the scale, these types of customers keep us on our toes and it helps us to learn and develop. They provide opportunities to grow and develop. We are more likely to build strong relationships with these types of customers because there is mutual respect – and we'll probably end up teaching each other something new. Servicing these accounts will be fun, challenging and rewarding.

At Point Z of the scale business becomes very cumbersome and life can be a misery. We lose sleep and we become de-motivated. In short, it's a distraction and you are better off without it.

Future

In planning our customer development we have to consider the future potential to grow and win additional business from the organizations that we choose to partner. If time and energy is dedicated to winning business we must consider whether a future exists in terms of:

- Can we sell more?
- Are there other subsidiaries or departments we can sell to?
- Is there a long-term relationship likely to develop?
- Are there opportunities to provide other products and services?

Some reminders on choosing customers

1. The best companies in the world choose their customers carefully
2. Avoid 'taking in washing'
3. Good customers build credibility
4. They are a great reference point
5. Bad customers usually equate to misery
6. Don't grab at business
7. Business will become easier and fun
8. Apply the 4F's screening tool

The future of an account can help us to direct our resource. If it is going to be a 'one hit wonder' then we should clearly think twice about how much time we devote to them.

FINDING THE DECISION MAKERS

In our forays into finding new customers we must, within the targeted organization, be clear on who's the real decision maker. Sometimes we may aim too high in an organization, maybe sometimes too low. It's about knowing where the balance of power lies and concentrating the right amount of effort on those individuals with influence.

Sometimes, of course, this is easier said than done. For example, if you are selling catering services to a blue chip publicly listed company, whilst it maybe useful to know the Chairman, it's unlikely that this particular decision will be down to him. You may be able to leverage his decision-making

---

Hitting the right pressure points

A client had experienced extensive problems in selling their electronic instrumentation to the chemicals industry. The equipment was designed to measure flow rates, temperatures and pressures in fairly harsh chemical environments. The sales manager spent enormous amounts of energy selling and trying to convince engineering teams in European plants to trial the equipment. Only after submission of detailed quotations did it become apparent that the team in Europe were a small part of a larger engineering and design unit of the US parent. After 6 months of hard graft, expensive trips, and design input it transpired that the New York technical department had the final say. No contact had been made with personnel in this Unit. This problem is symptomatic of other industries and is prevalent within many areas – IT solution providers face very similar problems.

---

capability but he is probably not the person you have to convince.

Other decision-making processes, such as those for high value goods or services will almost certainly be collective. Decision-making can often involve many different departments and individuals, all of whom may have a particular agenda, preference or inclination. This makes technical selling a complicated and often very protracted process primarily because you are dealing with:

- Different types of personalities
- Individuals with differing perspectives
- Individuals that may already have a personal relationship with other suppliers -possibly an incumbent provider that certain individuals within the decision making unit prefer to deal with
- Individuals that feel threatened, particularly if you are selling consultancy or advisory services

If, for example, you are selling radar systems to the aerospace sector you're often not only selling to the original equipment manufacturer but also, potentially, to other individuals within the supply chain. This could involve a mix of engineering, design, production/manufacturing and logistics personnel. It is not uncommon to find such complex structures in government and other public organizations. When dealing with major accounts where such complexity is highly apparent, we must take time to understand the 'pressure points' possessed by the primary decision makers.

The 'Pressure Point Matrix' encompasses three steps.

1. Identifying the primary decision makers

The starting point of the process is to obtain a clear understanding of the key individuals within your target organization. This can be arrived at through a number of fairly simple activities, which may include:

- Effective probing of the individuals assigned to brief you
- Internet search
- Gathering organizational charts for the target (these are readily available in the public sector)
- Making direct telephone calls to personnel or the department or customer you are targeting
- Asking suppliers or industry network groups

As part of this process it is vital to understand who would have a role to play and what their role may involve. If you are selling IT solutions and systems, whilst the primary contact is bound to be the IT Director, such a decision would never be made without consulting the other primary functions such as finance, sales, manufacturing, production, engineering or design. The chief executive and his or her other senior colleagues would also have a say.

Remember stakeholders could also involve specialists or experts such as consulting firms, lawyers, accountants or other advisors.

2. Prioritizing the decision makers

Once you've identified the key people you're looking to target you can map them onto the Pressure Point Matrix. The position in the matrix governs the way in which the individuals need to be tackled and approached.

- **'Hot Spots'** – these are primarily the individuals that have budget responsibility and are of primary importance to any business developer. These individuals control budgets and it is these decision makers that carry the maximum weight. They should be managed very closely and they're the ones that you have to impress. Remember, *your* personal credi-

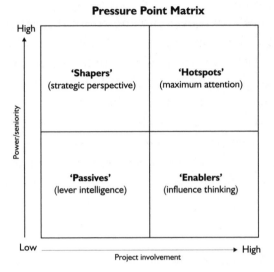

bility is at stake with the 'hot spots' so be sure that you satisfy them – you will only get one chance.

- **'Shapers'** – these are often the most senior individuals within an organization concerned with overall strategy and direction. These would typically be individuals whose day-to-day role would not involve them in your project; shapers tend to take a strategic perspective on a purchasing decision and would ensure that the decision is in the interest of the overall strategy, policy or direction of their business.

- **'Enablers'** – these are the project individuals that have a day-to-day high degree of involvement with projects and are usually junior management. Often they are part of a decision-making committee. For example if you are selling high specification analytical instrumentation to a multi national biotechnology company, whilst the R&D director may have ultimate decision making (i.e. the 'hot spot') his research team and day to day biochemists will have any enabling effect on the decision making. They must feel comfortable with the equipment – and, therefore you and your colleagues – because it affects their day-to-day role and job function.

- **'Passives'** – passives are the supporting personnel, frequently at administrative level, involved in projects. Care has to be taken with such individuals because they can often appear to be more influential than they really are. On the other hand, passives can be very effective mechanisms for finding in-company intelligence. Business developers use passives in a very strategic sense in that they are usually more accessible and can be used to impart knowledge on key decision makers, policy, strategies, personalities and needs.

Key tips on using the matrix

1. Use the Pressure Point Matrix to plot your current contacts in either existing or potential customers.

2. How well do you know the individuals in each quadrant – ask yourself honestly! Decide whom you need to get to know better.

3. Place the names in the quadrant using a colour system. Use 'green' for those you know well, 'amber' for those you need to know better and 'red' for those you don't know or you need to get closer to! 'Red' also represents those difficult characters that are proving to be difficult to build relationships with. The result of your plotting could be quite enlightening.

---

3. Understanding the decision makers

It is vital that we get to know more about the decision makers both professionally and emotionally:

- **Professionally** – What is their role and how do they approach their job and projects?
- **Emotionally** – How will they react to suggestions and

approaches? What makes them listen, tick and function as human beings?

We'll deal at a later stage with the psychology of the buying process and how you should read your customers and potential decision makers.

Here are some key questions that you need to ask yourself about these individuals:

- What type of personalities are you dealing with?
- What motivates them?
- What do they need from suppliers?
- Do they have an opinion of you or your company?
- What is the best way to approach them?
- Do they already have preferred suppliers?
- How are they viewed by the industry?
- What are their successes?
- What is the relationship between Shapers, Hot Spots, and Enablers and Passives?
- What budgets do they manage?
- Where do they sit on the fun index?
- What makes them tick and what are the buttons you need to press?

Think about your target customers in this light and ask yourself: Do you know what makes them tick?

PERSONAL NETWORKING

Personal networking – or, put another way, the ability to build effective professional relationships with both prospective customers and those individuals who influence purchasers to make decisions – has always been a core component within the skill set of a business developer.

But it's also true, however that over the years we've seen

what we'd call professional meeting attendees in action, but we've often questioned just how effective they were for their organization.

The key to networking in a business development and selling arena is that is puts you in a position to get in front of a customer that under normal circumstances would not happen. It's not just about eating sausage rolls and drinking wine, unfortunately! Building relationships is fine, but the key to success is establishing some objectives that you intend to secure at the end of the process; otherwise the only thing you might end up with is indigestion!

Whilst profile building and relationship enhancements are often vital by-products of networking, within the context of 'Pitch Perfect' – they should be used as sales lead generation tools, particularly in customer connectivity (in momentum building and functional mastery, networking has other important crossover such as building your personal brand and establishing a 'guru' image in your market). There are obvious links, but purchase orders are ultimately the end goal.

We can characterize our networks into three components, each with a direct impact on the connectivity process:

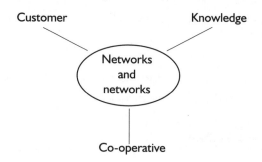

Customer networking/networks

This is very similar to leveraging those people that you directly know. However, customer networks could also include:

- Past customers

- Existing customers
- Overseas customers

Since you are already working with these organizations then ensure that opportunities to get together are initiated on a regular basis. These will encompass lunches, company events, corporate hospitality, and award ceremonies. The personal touch is always an effective way of leveraging existing and past customer networks. The lunch meeting is always a good way of getting information on customer potential.

Knowledge networks

Don't ignore the knowledge networks that exist – they can provide an important source of what is going on at a macro level. Government bodies, trade organizations, regulatory bodies, industry bodies, professional practices, banks etc can all provide vital clues as to where markets and customers are going and who is doing what. This can help when we hit the brick wall of lead generation. Introductions can sometimes help to redirect our efforts. Don't forget suppliers either – A vital source of potential customers.

Co-operative networks

We will go on to see how alliances and partnerships are becoming an important part of winning new business. By teaming up with organizations with complementary skills access to new opportunities can emerge. Networking with these organizations can be a source of new lead generation and customer possibilities. Some common examples of co-operation networks would be interior designers working with commercial developers, PR agencies working with advertising agencies, management consultancies working with publishers – there are many more. These co-operative arrangements should not be overlooked as they can often open the big door!

List your networks

Networks	Who are they? List them
Customer	•
Knowledge	•
Co-operation	•

GETTING UNDER THE SKIN – BEING PREPARED

Looking at life from their point of view

Never forget that you must always put yourself in the buyer's shoes and ask yourself what is in it for them. The psychology of this process involves the purchaser thinking, "How and why should I give you my time?" That is why, prior to any meeting, we must consider the following points:

- What is motivating the buyer?
- How can I make a difference?
- What can I 'give' to make it worthwhile for them?
- What examples can I provide of relevance to them?

This mindset is not always prevalent in our thinking and often selling is confused with what can be gained without any giving. This is a big mistake – it *has* to be a win for them and a win for you!

Put yourself in the buyer's shoes and ask yourself:
what would I want?

It's critically important to understand the organizational and purchasing dynamics you're dealing with. You must be able to drill down to obtain the information that provides both qualitative and quantitative feedback on a target customer's needs – both explicit in their brief and implicit in their emotional positioning. Being armed with this information is crucial since it provides you with both an intimate understanding of their needs and an effective defence against any objections they may have.

Getting under the skin of a client helps prepare for any likely objections.

Here are some of the stages you'll need to drill to:

- **Level One**: **organizational dynamics**   Are they a good customer to be associated with?
- **Level Two: purchasing dynamics**   How do they buy?
- **Level Three: understanding their personality**   Are we sure we understand their psyche?

Level One: organizational dynamics

The first step in the process is to establish as much information as you can about the target's organizational values, their culture and their strategic direction. This will help you to ascertain how your potential customer operates and deals with its suppliers. It is, indeed, indicative of their business ethics, and will help you to answer our 4Fs challenge.

Drilling down for customer information

You should also do your homework by digging in other directions. Here's a checklist – see what you can establish:

- Financial accounts
- Searching through press articles and media information
- Annual reports

- Product brochures and leaflets
- Websites
- Talking to suppliers and industry movers & shakers
- Visiting exhibitions

Level Two: purchasing dynamics

At this stage of the process, we equip ourselves with more in-depth information on their procurement policy, practices and strategies. At this point you might want to go back to the Pressure Point Matrix as it is the individuals that you've plotted on to this chart that help you to understand the decision making practices that exist within the targeted organization. Gathering influential information at this point will come from:

- Talking to shapers, hot spots and enablers
- Leveraging knowledge from passives
- Talking to suppliers
- Conducting discussions with trade representatives

A systematic approach to gathering customer intelligence is vital. Some companies commission market research to gather some of this information; others use telephone and face-to-face discussions to review, analyse and question purchasing and decision-making personnel.

A structured technique to information gathering also helps to plan and focus your offer to meet your target customer's needs. It will also help you because it will:

- Produce vital background on the target, their culture and organizational values
- Facilitate a structured approach to how you take your planning forward
- Demonstrate to the target that care has been taken in understanding their needs, aspirations and problems
- Enhance your credibility

- Ensure that your approach is not 'me too'

This approach will also help you anticipate any potential objections that a target customer may throw at you when you apprise them of your proposed solution. After all, a key factor to successful selling is to prevent or at least anticipate objections prior to a sales pitch or business presentation. The systematic approach put forward here will help you build an information base that positions you very favourably in negotiations – it puts you on the front foot from the start.

By thoroughly preparing and diagnosing many of the key issues prior to any detailed discussion taking place, most if not all of the barriers to securing a sale are overcome early in negotiations.

Level Three: understanding their personality

There is a further level of drilling that can be incredibly effective. Here, what we're trying to do is to build an understanding of the personality of the decision maker before we meet them. Although we'll deal with the psychology of selling in latter sections, it's worth raising at this stage as it can prove to be highly beneficial if we know the type or personality of the person we are dealing with before the meeting.

Ask advice on what your prospect is like and what their approach may be. It's feasible to ask colleagues, suppliers and peers how well they know the individuals in question – this again helps you to prepare and deploy an approach that dovetails with the clients' psyche or general personality/approach. Here are some tips:

Preparation, preparation, preparation

It sounds like a statement of the obvious but if you don't prepare, you don't deserve to succeed.

The 6 P's Mantra is a business cliché, but it's worth saying that most sayings get to become clichés because there's a fair degree of truth in them. For those of you unfamiliar with this little ditty, here it is, with some subtle editing for the more sensitive reader.

P   **Prior**
P   **Planning**
P   **Prevents**
P   **Pathetically (or some other Anglo-Saxon word of your choice!)**
P   **Poor**
P   **Performance**

Planning is a widely used term in all walks of business, but it's easy to under-estimate the level of preparation that is required to achieve a positive result.

Preparation is often seen as wasted time and all too often it is tempting to just *wing* it. There should be no surprise when short-cutting the business development process ends in failure.

If you're to help build a successful business, the best customers are the ones that are worth working towards winning. Take time to gather information and ensure that the prospects you want to do business with add value to your operations and activity. Interestingly enough, the process of gathering information on prospective customers will also help you to decide whether you should be doing business with them. You'll get to know each other, and a lot of ground will be tested in the meantime – enough opportunity to establish that all important feel good factor – or, conversely, plenty of chances for the warning bells to ring.

Over and above this, when engagement eventually takes place with customers, a sound understanding of their needs and aspirations should have been acquired. This paves the way for effective business development to take place, which is:

- Focused and directed
- Based on sound information

- Meeting a customer's needs and requirements
- Well positioned to succeed
- Creating the platform for mutually beneficial corporate strategies to be developed

REACHING CUSTOMERS

As we've already said, there's a plethora of techniques available to business development professionals looking to reach customers.

Marketing – advertising and PR, exhibitions, event based marketing, demonstrations, texting to mobiles, company open days, social and sporting events, and corporate entertainment –

Ten ideas for reaching your customers

1. Use a text alert service to customers telling them of your offer (estate agents are using this as 80% of the population now own a mobile)
2. Hold a customer conference/open day and get it hosted by a top personality
3. Write a book and use it as the basis of a mailer to your targeted customers
4. Enter into email debate with targeted individuals
5. Put a CD together of your offer and use it as part of a mailer. Make it interactive
6. Use viral marketing to spread the message
7. Forget the brochure. Construct a poster and distribute it to customers
8. Try PR and advertising – ask for creative inputs from agencies
9. Exhibit at a leading industry trade fair. Let all your customers know you are going. (Use ideas 6, 7 and 8 to support the activity)
10. Take specialist advice on increasing hits to your website

---

may well all fall within your remit, and, to reinforce the point, it's your responsibility to go and find out more about how each of these disciplines actually work.

In many respects, it's not the choosing of the technique that is important here. What's more important is that you put in place a process that helps you to concentrate your efforts on the most appropriate marketing techniques that is suited to your marketplace, offer, budget and culture.

The RIP technique is a useful way to think about maximizing the chances of gaining a foothold in the targeted customer's door. RIP can be applied to any aspect of lead generation activity – it basically states that you should **R**esearch, **I**nnovate and **P**lan when a new customer development initiative is being considered.

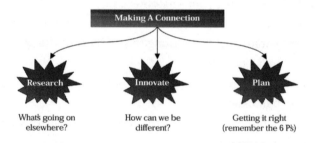

Whether it's an exhibition or company open day, a direct mail campaign or a public relations programme, you should be able to prove to yourself and your colleagues precisely why the route you've chosen stacks up.

Here are some hints to help you through the process.

Research

- What are your competitors doing in addition to the activity you are considering?
- How do they reach their customers?
- What activities are used in other industries or markets?
- What tools do they use?
- Think about comparable or totally different sectors. If you

are in the international services market, can
lead generation tools be applied from the
retail sector?

Think laterally about the best routes

Innovate

- How will you attract *attention* with your chosen activity?
- Make the offer exciting so that *interest* is aroused and the targeted individual wants to find out more
- The interest should initiate a *desire* to take *action* to proceed with further discussions

Doing something different that will arouse attention. You will get noticed!

Planning

- Be sure that the timing of your initiative does not coincide with any conflicting activity or initiatives
- Be sure that the target audience has been well thought through (think about the pressure point matrix)
- Could your activity dovetail with a particular event (e.g. a major exhibition) or an ideal time in your customer's calendar, e.g. end of year accounting period where there is money left in the budget?
- Be sure that any lead generation activity is part of a co-ordinated plan of marketing support. In the vast majority of cases, one-off initiatives waste money

Always remember the 6 P's

- Sustainable ongoing lead generation activity pays dividends. Trying it once and failing is not evidence to say it does not work

FILTERING THE LEADS

This is where fear can set in for many business developers. Picking up the phone and asking for a meeting or whether someone received information makes many of us feel uncomfortable.

Well, it's a fact of life that many experienced developers

don't like to do this! Wearing out the shoe leather is a key component of the selling process. However you can only do that once you have an appointment to attend. The process we have described in this section includes:

- Picking up the phone and asking for the appointment
- Assessing levels of interest
- Diarying a meeting date

Filtering the leads ensures qualification of a lead and that time is worthwhile spending with a potential budget holder or decision maker.

CREATING A CUSTOMER ROAD MAP

The route to finding new customers should be viewed as a journey. In the same way as we plan a trip, the destination to securing discussions with new prospects requires:

- A starting point
- A recognition of the landmarks on the way
- Contingency plans for a diversion
- An expected timescale
- A budget to make the journey
- Arrival

Use the roadmap as a way of visualizing the activities that need to be undertaken to take you from where you are now to where you want to go.

It's also fundamentally important not only to work out where you want to go, but why you want to get there. Many large organizations seeking to buy from people like you are keen to establish whether their supplier partners understand their own differentiation and vision – so it's critical that you invest a high degree of strategic thought within this process.

Creating your own roadmap will help you visualize the milestones you'll need to pass in order to be successful. Think about the following points as a starter:

- What is the customer trying to achieve?
- How do the products/services you offer fit?
- Is there alignment between what you offer and what they want?
- How are you different?

Once you have answered these questions then you are in a position to think through the steps that need to be taken in order to gain an entree to those targeted customers. The roadmap will assist in understanding what needs to be achieved:

The customer roadmap

FINDING CUSTOMERS – HINTS AND TIPS

- Don't make assumptions – 80% of your opportunities will be hidden beneath the surface
- Trust intuition and follow your hunches. Experience goes a long way
- Leverage your existing contacts
- Don't grab at business – the stuff you grab could well be unprofitable
- Review your targeted customer websites – these contain vital purchasing information

- Remember wherever to 'ask for advice'. People will help to point you in the right direction
- Choose your customers – 4 F's
- Make sure you are talking to the complete decision maker units – apply the 'pressure point' thinking
- Remember that information gathering is about drilling down the levels. This avoids making assumptions
- Research the personalities of the people you are targeting. Understanding emotional needs goes a long way. You are then prepared before you go through the door!
- 6 P's will help you prepare well for objections
- Reaching customers means that you must do something different, innovative and exciting.
- Apply the RIP technique
- Visualize and draw your customer roadmap. This will help you understand how to get that all important first meeting

CHAPTER 8

Winning the Business

"So, after reviewing your credentials and meeting the team last week, we'd like you to put together your proposals that will meet our requirements".

Even if you've been in the business development profession for a long time, you should never get tired of hearing words like these.

Here's *your* chance to put your plans into action and secure that major new contract. Here's *your* chance to go out there – and win.

> The language of modern selling is not "What do you require and how can we sell it to you? It is: "where are you going and how can we help you get there?
>
> *Robin Fielder, sales and management guru*

What happens next is, of course, the key to the process. Securing new business involves the effective use of all our interpersonal skills married with tried and tested tools that will ensure impact is achieved with buyers and decision makers.

Winning business model

Winning business involves the effective selling of yourself, the company you're representing and the products and services on offer. To make this count, you'll need to be able to build upon all of the 'Pitch Perfect' principles and demonstrate credibility through functional mastery & passion, personal drive, momentum, and positive attitude to achievement.

In today's selling environment, there are many tools at our disposal to ensure that when we are engaging with customers we:

- Excite them
- Create an overwhelming desire for them to choose our products/services
- Ensure objectives are met head on
- Instil the confidence that our offer is the best
- Deliver to a high degree of satisfaction

In this section we review the most appropriate methods for winning business and creating the right level of impact.

REVISITING THE CONNECTIVITY SPECTRUM

Don't forget, that as we've already said, there are different points at which we can potentially connect with prospective customers. It will be different on each occasion, but essentially, these stages comprise:

- An enquiry
- Clearance of pre-qualifications, where appropriate
- A first meeting to explore customer needs
- An invitation to pitch
- The pitch creation process
- The presentation and/or submission

There's no doubt that this multi-stage selling process can absorb significant energy, resources and time – but the rewards make it worthwhile. It's also a process that will call upon all our functional mastery skills. In the majority of instances you will be selling:

- Solutions offered by your products and services
- Your company capability/track record and history
- Differentiation
- Your knowledge of the market
- You!

What is key to this process is recognizing the 'bonding agents' that can to be applied so that you're able to lock into the prospective customer's thinking. These can be summarized in the following table:

Connection Point	Bonding Agent
Enquiry and Pre-qualification	• Respond with material specific to needs of clients • Avoid 'me too' cut and paste letters. Treat the enquiry as unique • Ensure that any pre-qualification becomes a professionally handled formality
First Date	• Telephone call first to assess needs • Try to understand the type of people you are dealing with • Take examples and case studies • Listen attentively; ask intelligent questions; remember that you're on show and you're already being 'scored'
Getting on Tender Lists	• Provide comprehensive company information • Avoid 'me too' material • Provide evidence of success and impact • Provide examples of satisfied clients

Pitch Preparation	• Plan effectively; build a team; delegate according to strengths
	• Prepare; Thunderbolt, Brainstorm, sift, select, edit, check
	• Clearly state your understanding of the issue
	• Make your pitch look different, visual, CD's
	• Avoid 'cut and paste'
	• Differentiate the offer
	• Use novel ways of presenting if it's the right thing to do
Presentation	• Exercise bravery
	• Use the Treasure Chest
	• Words, pictures and sound
	• Rehearse, rehearse, rehearse
	• Anticipate objections
	• Give ideas freely
	• Provide strategic paper and handouts prior to presentation

We'll go onto explore in more detail how these bonding agents can be applied so that you're making the best possible contact with the prospective customers you're targeting.

There is, however, one key thought that should stay with you throughout this process:

How can we add value for the customer?

You'll need to use this as your touchstone thought whenever you're working on any stage of the winning process.

FIRST IMPRESSIONS REALLY COUNT

We'd pretty much agree with the view you've got ten seconds in which to make a good first impression with a potential customer. Whilst this maybe the case, it's essential that you give consideration to the 6P Preparation rule tool. Here, ask yourself:

■   Who are you going to see?

- What are they like as people, personalities and professionals?
- What they are really looking for – and does this stack up against what they're actually saying?

Provide effective answers to these questions, and you'll have a better than average chance of engaging with prospective customers and making the right first impression.

In simple terms, a telephone conversation to understand the emphases they're placing on a written brief should help you to prepare your case and not only generate sufficient information upon which to make a sensible connection with the client, but also for you to start shaping your battle plan. Simple questioning techniques should aim to establish expectations and for an initial pitch to be made to:

- Demonstrate that you understand their broad requirements
- Identify the areas of your offer that are particularly pertinent to their needs
- Highlight the support information that they may find beneficial
- Establish the ground rules of engagement

Whilst this may seem extremely basic, it does actually happen to

---

A thought-horror story

Have you ever turned up to a meeting when you were only expecting to meet one person – or worse still, you'd kind of assumed that they'd only field one person, but you'd not really stopped to think about it first? You walk through the door and there's a crowd of people standing there! What a dreadful – and avoidable – experience!

---

the most successful of business developers. A simple call could have ensured that this didn't take place.

Key message

Try and avoid surprises that may shock. This applies both ways.

Don't forget, too, that this is a two-way street, but as the prospective supplier, the onus falls to you to take the lead and brief the prospect on how *you* intend to handle your side of the meeting.

Your role, and a colleague's role within a meeting needs to be clearly articulated to prospective customers.

PSYCHOLOGY OF SELLING

In selling low value items, engaging personally with an individual is not always as important as with high value projects. Why? In low value selling, individuals are typically looking for the best deal and more often than not no follow-on relationship is needed once the transaction has been made.

Do not forget the importance of selling the intangible – a relationship!
John Leach

Conversely, in larger value sales situations involving significant capital expenditure, there will invariably be many client visits after the transaction has been made.

Engaging psychologically

The bigger the value the deal, the more important it is to engage psychologically with your customer. Here's a story to illustrate how this happens.

Engaging psychologically is the starting point of any relationship. Get this wrong and there's every chance that you'll miss out on the sale. It's vital that you recognize at your first meeting the type of person that you are dealing with, and if you fail to engage and empathize then recovery is very difficult.

There are many techniques designed to read and understand personality types. With experience you'll begin to read

---

Making the connection

A company director needed to buy a new desk for his home study. He also needed to specify a major new accounts package for his business. It just so happened that he had to sort both purchases on one day.

First – the desk. The sales executive was smugness personified. Nevertheless, the director realized that the desk was a good deal, so he went ahead with the purchase.

Later that afternoon, a sales manager from a major financial software business came to see the MD about the new accounts package that would require an investment approaching £150,000. The sales manager was friendly, and painted a broadbrush picture of the kind of thing that his company could achieve. After one hour the MD closed the meeting and indicated that although he had enjoyed their conversation he would not be taking the enquiry any further.

Why did the sales manager blow it?

He failed to recognize the prospective customer was a dominant person who was looking for factual information and specific examples of how the system had benefited other clients.

The director realized that not only was he buying a system, he was also buying a relationship with the sales manager who would need to return on a number of occasions.

What the sales manager failed to realize was that he was selling a 'relationship' – A fundamental aspect of any complex, high value, sale that involves high degrees of aftercare.

The director would have far rather gone for a beer with the software guy than the desk guy, but he bought from the desk guy because that deal meant far less to him.

---

body language and personality types intuitively. One school defines personality traits in the business context into four categories:

- Dominant
- Influential
- Steady
- Compliant

Of course, many people possess a mix of these traits. Whilst this may be the case, there are some rough guidelines that we can follow depending on our initial analysis of our prospect's personality. If we identify then choose the right emotional approach then our chances of success are far greater. Remember:

In complex consultative sales, customers buy relationships first.

The following table will help you to understand the best approach to take with your prospect. If you can assess beforehand the types then this will help you to prepare.

If your prospect is	Then remember to
A **Dominant** person they may: • be extremely confident and verbally very articulate • come across as forceful • appear assertive, if not a little aggressive	• prepare with factual information • let them take the lead • provide specific examples of how similar people have been serviced • provide personal testimonials • leave lots of personal space
An **Influential** person may be: • friendly and animated • fairly relaxed and loud • conversational in approach • like creative ideas • expressive	• use fun as an approach • not be afraid of entering their space • use visual support • show motivation • make them look good if they purchase
A **Steady** type of person is likely • to be very detailed and methodical • relaxed with an emotionless style • dislike confrontation • soft voiced and monitored	• emphasize guarantees • don't interrupt • listen carefully

A **Compliant** person then they
- are precise
- cool, perhaps aloof
- reserved in their body language
- low risk takers
- very direct in approach and eye contact

- provide facts and data
- anticipate lots of questions, so prepare thoroughly
- don't expose them to risk
- don't be too personal
- don't invade their space

ENGAGEMENT

You'll start to build engagement once effective introductions have been made and a potential customer enjoys a good first impression. Successful engagements reflect the fact that an initial review of your offer makes sense to your potential customer; however, there are a number of caveats to this point.

You'll also have to prove that you, your products/services and your company are:

- Decent
- Honest
- True
- Committed

By doing your homework well, entering a pre-meeting dialogue, and providing relevant, credibility building examples, you'll convey your belief in the products and services you are offering – which is key to our principles of possessing strong personal values and ethics.

The best business developers:

- Establish rapport and insight
- Understand needs
- Anticipate objections
- Avoid selling on the hoof
- Ensure that a potential customer sees real value in discussing issues with them

Building a structured approach

There is no short cut to understanding the needs of customers. A structured approach to developing new contacts can, however, offer a 'faster than usual' entry to new business.

Capturing the attention of the prospective customer is the key first stage of this approach. The primary challenge from this point is to ensure that this attention is maintained throughout the subsequent stages of progressing the lead to purchase order.

These subsequent stages are captured in the following diagram. The interest stage is created through active listening and questioning to build a more detailed knowledge of the prospect's specific needs.

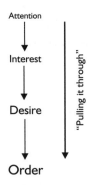

How do you go about building interest into desire? The Desire element of engagement is stimulated when your offer demonstrates real value and benefit to a client's situation or when it solves a particular problem or challenge they may have.

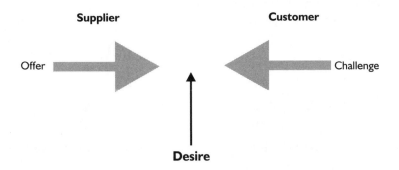

Sounds good, doesn't it? Well it does, but although you shouldn't really lose a tender opportunity if you've created strong desire, here comes a further word of caution…

Don't be a busy fool!

In consultative selling there is always the danger of prospects searching for free ideas.

Here's a sorry tail we heard recently following a conversation with a company that sold ticketing solutions:

Here is a busy fool

"We helped the design team develop the specification for a new system. Days upon days of free time were committed to supporting the engineering team. The final spec was placed to tender and we lost on price!"

Clearly there will always be occasions when this happens. Nevertheless, there are several tips you might want to consider to reduce the risk of this happening:

Some tips

1. Use the pressure point matrix – are you talking to the decision makers?
2. Understand clearly the emotional/psychology individuals involved in the decision-making
3. Check what the budget is for
4. Be clear on who owns the intellectual property
5. Do the 4 F's apply?
6. Ask if they are discussing the project with others
7. Explain clearly that you want the job

DATA GATHERING – GETTING THE DETECTIVE WORK RIGHT

Whether they're real-life cops or TV 'tecs, there's one thing that investigative police officers excel at – and that's good old-fashioned detective work.

You must get on the prospect's case and research and record the key facts that you'll need in order to prepare yourself – *and* decide if a certain customer is worthy of attention.

Much of this work can be carried out through desk and telephone research; many business development professionals are often surprised how much information and data can be gathered through what are fairly simple methods. Much of the specific contract information that you'll need, however, can only be truly gleaned through 'face to face' discussions with potential clients.

Working on hard evidence means ensuring that you have covered the ground and that your actions are built upon solid foundations. If you can satisfy yourself that you have:

- Spoken to all the stakeholders
- Asked pertinent questions about budgets
- Built a working relationship with decision makers

Then you'll be taking many of the right steps towards winning the work.

The figure on the next page shows a mind map – a way that Strategem captures key information in an easy-to-digest format. Try creating a mind map for yourself to plot out the key areas of detail that you'll need to turn your next pitch into a real winning opportunity.

The one we've created here is by no means exhaustive; it merely demonstrates some of the data that you'll probably need to gather so that you can make some big decisions as you prepare your planning.

So that you don't waste time on what could become an

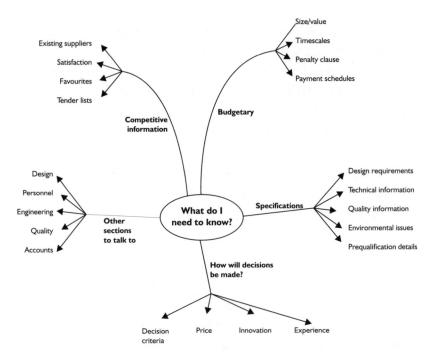

unviable pitch, this process will also help you answer the following questions:

- Is there a real opportunity?
- Is it financially viable?
- Are there incumbent suppliers?
- Can we compete?
- What differentiators need to be applied?
- Do we want the business?

Remember that functional mastery plays an important role in this data-gathering phase. Excelling in functional mastery ensures that you are asking the right questions of a potential customer. If you are not sure then take a colleague to a meeting.

Uncomfortable Questions
It's a fact of life that none of us enjoy pursuing tough lines of enquiry. But it's also true that the best business development pro-

fessionals often show their mettle in their ability to ask uncomfortable questions.

At the end of the day, you *will* need to ask these questions if the prospect doesn't volunteer the information:

- What is your budget?
- Who else are you talking to?
- Who are your current suppliers?
- Is the pitch really up for grabs?
- When will you make a decision?

Ask that uncomfortable question!

An effective business developer will ensure that they're going to ask the right questions prior to making a visit to a prospective customer. Involving other colleagues might help here, as they will undoubtedly possess a different perspective to help round out your interrogative approach.

Tips on data gathering
1. Mind map what you need to know
2. Get input from your team
3. Show your customer the mind map you have put together – they'll love it!
4. Read all relevant background information you have obtained
5. Look at the client's website prior to meeting
6. Ask the 'uncomfortable' question

PROBING AND LISTENING

But this process is more than just asking. It's also about listening.

Learn to listen well. It's actually not as easy as it sounds, and it also takes a good deal of concentration. Think about your favourite news radio journalist. When they're interviewing a politician, they're not just asking questions; they're listening intently to the answers that they're given...so that they can amend their next question – and possibly the ones that follow.

If you don't listen, and don't take notes, you'll forget key details very quickly. Practise this with your colleagues so that you don't make this mistake when you're with prospects. Don't forget that in complex selling environments information is *key* and in many instances it is vital to discuss requirements with more than one individual. It often requires meetings with other departments or functions and debate with a wide range of stakeholders – shapers, hot spots, enablers and passives. Possessing good questioning, listening and recording skills will help you get under the skin of the prospect and help you assess their needs well.

Quite simply, probing for information means that asking sensible, well-informed questions should be followed by a period of listening to ensure that we capture and record a prospect's:

- Problems
- Challenges
- Project ideas
- Desires
- Call for help

An ability to listen intently is a key component of relationship building. In Customer Connectivity it can be the difference between winning and losing. Listening is at the heart of effective communication. Listening well helps us to understand problems then analyse ways of improving or adding value.

Remember our pen pictures of some typical business development traits? Well, the Rough Diamond just wants to make the sale and isn't really interested in the prospect or their needs.

The Crashing Bore is only interested in telling the customer about how much he knows about the product. Conversely, the Steady Eddies and Winners are keen to please and their selling approach comes from the heart. Their desire to listen is an intrinsic element of the way they think and operate. Their customer caring nature of these individuals creates engagement with customers.

The ability to listen is crucial to showing interest
and a desire to support

Here are some facts for you to digest. Most people can speak at around 2-3 words per second – so when we're on the receiving end, we're listening to around 150 words per minute. If we're listening, how much of this do you think we're actually retaining? On average, you'd be lucky to surpass 30%, and only through practice and concentration will this go much higher.

Knowledge speaks but wisdom listens
Jimi Hendrix

And, thinking about it, that's true if *you're* doing the talking, which has significant implications for how *you* should package your thoughts, ideas, inputs and views when communicating with a prospective customer.

The message here is: listen attentively, and choose your own words carefully to ensure that your audience is in the best possible position to hear your key points.

Active listening stages
1. Listen to what is being said and try to avoid the surroundings and other distractions
2. Evaluate what is being said and then respond only when there is something sensible to be said
3. Ask those strategic questions that you need answers to. Refer back our 'getting the facts' mind map
4. Avoid interruptions at all costs

This aspect of the selling process is a prime illustration of how functional mastery – our knowledge – needs to work in harmony with Customer Connectivity – our ability to engage. It is best summed up in the quotation from Oliver Wendell Holmes (American physician, poet and essayist).

It is the province of knowledge to speak and it is the privilege of wisdom to hear
Oliver Wendell Holmes

Whilst for many enthusiastic business developers listening can be a major challenge, to obtain excellence in this area is a lesson must be learnt from the greatest entrepreneurs – These are active listeners!

RECORDING

The art of listening, talking and writing for many can be an extremely difficult process to manage. However, recording what has been said in meetings is vital because invariably most, follow up involves putting together a written response based on the data that has been gleaned. Here mind mapping has a most valuable role to play. Those that practise this method of recording information would claim it has had a dramatic effect on their success not only in understanding the problem or client issue but also in securing business and new customers. It is a technique that Strategem has used widely not only in its own business development efforts but also in our coaching of senior managers.

Recording information using words, symbols, pictures and colour dramatically increases our creativity and retention of information. Taking notes by use of mind maps also dramatically speeds up our creative thinking process and problem solving capability. The mind mapping technique makes use of both the left side of the brain (logical/analytical) with that of the right side (creative and inspirational). By combining both sides of the brain, note taking and recording of information becomes enjoyable and far more effective. As this technique is practised it becomes an invaluable tool for problem solving and idea generation during meetings.

How to mind map

1. Use the centre of the notebook
2. Use a word or a picture/symbol as the central theme
3. Use colours where possible
4. Connect each theme to the central image using trunk lines
5. Sub themes and key points can then branch from each connecting trunk
6. Use key words
7. Use images
8. Practice until you develop the technique to suit your own particular style

The example opposite shows the way in which we mind mapped a fast growth programme for newly formed businesses.

Like any other new approach, Mind Mapping takes time, and effort before it becomes a strong part of your arsenal, but, with practice, you'll find that note taking becomes fun. We've found that once you get good at it, you'll want to use it in other elements of your business development process, including:

planning	customer mapping	intelligence gathering
idea generation	breakthrough selling ideas	how to differentiate your offer
personal development	presenting ideas	selling tools, ideas
making presentations	selling ideas	personal improvement

It Really Works!!

OBJECTIONS – DISPELLING THE MYTHS

If you've ever be tempted to buy an old school sales guide, you won't have failed to notice a section in there that's called something like "Overcome That Objection!" or "Close That Sale!"

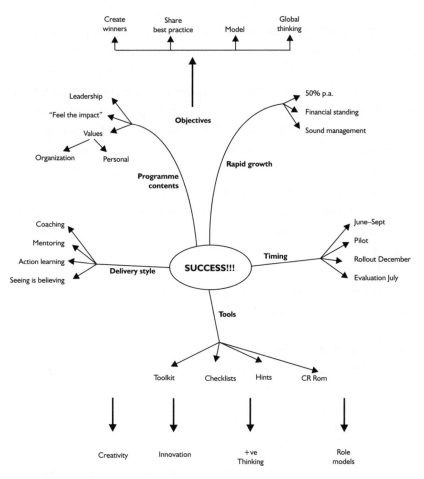

Example Notes taken from the discussion with a client looking to develop a 'fast growth' coaching programme

In other words, whatever the doubts, fears or queries a potential customer may possess, your job is to get the signature on the contract, come what may.

How much of this advice possesses merit, and how much could be viewed as trickery? Could it be said that what you're really doing is placing a person in a buying position when in reality they do not want to be there?

> I can't think of anything worse than selling someone something they don't want.
> *Julian Richer, Richer Sounds*

If business development is to move on to a more collaborative, consultative, consensual basis, then it must learn that skill of 'objection prevention' as opposed to 'objection overcoming'.

Getting under the skin of client's problems and effective preparation married with the functional mastery skills provide excellent ammunition to counteract a buyer's concerns. Functional mastery skills, exemplified by an intimate corporate knowledge, and an understanding of your own offer, the competition and the market environment help to minimize the chances of the prospect holding a clutch of objections.

It's a cliché, but forewarned is forearmed, particularly in the field of preventing objections becoming a barrier to winning business.

We've found that deploying an Objections Map can help discipline the way in which we identify and root out issues before they crop up and block our way.

Objections map – the steps

1. Bring together a team of people from your organization that represents the various functions and processes within your organization
2. Define the issue in simple terms – "what might stop this prospective customer from buying from us?"
3. Hold a brainstorming session to review progress to date and to discuss the issues and obtain responses
4. Group the answers in the format as shown in the next figure.
5. Review in detail each of the issues that emerge from the objections map and think about how to respond (write down the appropriate response to the objections)

This approach not only helps us to prepare well, but also contributes to ongoing improvement and developments of the 'offer' that we make within the market place. It can additionally highlight:

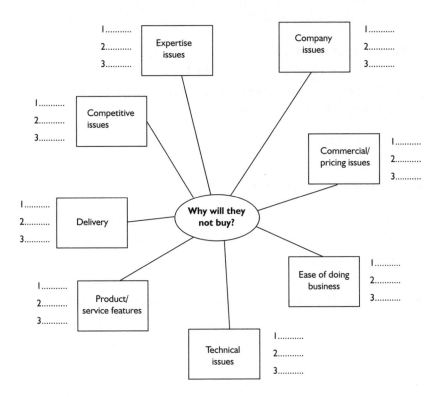

- Customer service problems
- Product development requirements
- Personnel problems
- Training issues
- Production/engineering challenges
- Pricing terms and other commercial problems
- Delivery issues
- Quality
- Product specification and improvements

For each of the objections identified it is important to write down how you would respond to the objections in question. So, if or when customers present these objections you can answer authoritatively and with passion borne out of conviction and understanding.

> **Put this in your toolkit**
> Research by Huthwaite's Neil Rackham identified that the world's best business developers focus on 'objection prevention' rather than objection 'overcoming'

FEEDING BACK YOUR IDEAS

The consultative sell requires a regular 'toing and froing' of ideas and suggestions of the way a product/service can bring value or benefit to a customer. Presenting ideas can be:

- *Proactively generated* by business developers to encourage a customer to take onboard your products or services. These prove important when sowing seeds with prospective customers
- *Reactively generated* by business developers in direct response to a particular project or activity that the customer is seeking to engage the services of a supplier

Remember, it's not *that* unusual for you to target a prospective client rather than simply wait for them to contact you and ask you to tender. It's here where the generation of proactive ideas is particularly useful. It could well be that there may not be a budget or immediate buying need but there is genuine interest or possibility of a contract in the future. However there is a definite potential to make a sale.

This sales incubation period is the time from when your messages start to reach customers and up to the point when they

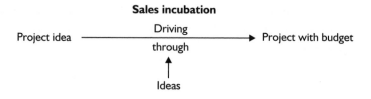

take action. You can speed up the process by documenting thoughts, opinions and suggestions.

In the consultative sales environment, sales incubation periods can be quite long; big-ticket projects require persistence and patience to pull through. Studies in the United States have shown that 75% of corporate prospects with active buying intentions make purchases six months after contact has been initiated, and in 58% of cases, this incubation period stretches to over a year.

Getting it on paper

In such situations it is vital that efforts are focused and ideas should be presented in a concise and simple way that will attract attention and facilitate discussions. It is part of the pulling through process. Again mind mapping can be used here to present ideas effectively, clearly and without too much trouble. An ideas mind map can be generated fairly easily and cost effectively, and it also provides an excellent framework on which to discuss and debate ideas and possibilities. A properly constructed mind map with colour and visuals does actively help to drive forward debate and decision/progression of ideas into potential contracts. An example of a mind map system Strategem constructed for a set of clients is shown on the next page (in black and white). This depicts the ideas from the staging of an entrepreneurial development initiative.

Other ways of proactively generating or feeding back ideas is through concept papers, ideas booklets, ideas papers or information booklets. Some examples include:

- *Lawyers* Put together booklets on issues such as intellectual property, forming a company, legal agreements
- *Accountants* Develop fact sheets on taxation, management buyouts, writing a business plan
- *Freight forwarders* Produce fact sheets on doing business abroad, transport and logistics

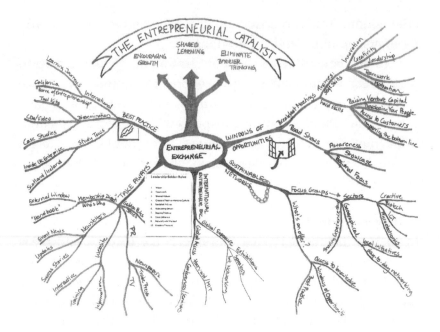

Such organizations produce these fact sheets and booklets in order to demonstrate to their prospective and existing clients that they are experts in their given arena. They provide customers with sufficient information, then hopefully capture business through a clear demonstration of functional mastery.

Although such tools prove to be highly valuable in the consultative selling environment, care has to be taken that just the right amount of information is provided without giving away the 'crown jewels'.

Think about your own technical / functional competency and services. Could a booklet or ideas paper be prepared in order to position the company as highly knowledgeable and credible?

In a situation where ideas have to be presented in response to a particular project, contract or programme, it is vital to keep information to a readable length, i.e. not too much. Such ideas paper should follow a well thought through, clear, concise and logical format that identifies:

- An understanding of the current situation?
- What needs to be achieved?

- Actions needed to achieve the desired outcome
- Positive outputs/outcomes
- Timings and outline budgets

This could be fed back in no more than two sheets of A4 paper, normally presented as a series of summary points and which covers the key issues and components of the offer.

WINNING PROPOSALS

In the vast majority of cases, professional business developers will need to prepare a pitch or proposal, frequently backed up by a face-to-face formal presentation, to acquire a contract or secure a project.

Such pitches are usually competitive and can involve the client reviewing the competing solutions of a number of potential providers. There are a number of guidelines that should be followed in order to ensure that *your* pitch stands out from the crowd.

But before we look at how you might approach the challenge, here's an easy way to damage your chances of winning. Simply cut and paste an old proposal and try to flog it to the next prospect. With today's computing capability, this technological sleight of hand is quick and cheap – the only trouble is, it looks it too.

A structured approach to pitch writing
- Pitch strategy
- Proposal strategy
- Proposal structure
- Draft
- Edit and review
- Assemble, check and deliver

While time pressures can mean that it's often tempting to put forward 'me too' pitches that are based on previous documents prepared, such an approach stifles creativity and innovation. Well thought through and differentiated pitches require time and effort to prepare. They are time consuming to put together and often acquire inputs from personnel at the most senior levels within companies – but if the deal's worth winning, it's worth going the extra mile.

Pitch strategy – go for it or don't bother? The big picture

Following a request to tender, your first step should be to seek a meeting with your prospective client to investigate further their needs and how they see the world. Key questions to address during this pitch strategy planning stage include:

- How big is the opportunity?
- Do we really have a chance of winning?
- Is the time and effort worthwhile?
- Do we have the capacity to fulfil the contract?
- Are partnerships required?
- Who will write the pitch?

Asking these questions enables you to clarify whether a pitch should be prepared and whether commercially and strategically it fits within your company's plan and purpose. Does it make sense to pitch? Would pitching put you in a position to secure other possible tenders or contracts? Whilst you might not win this time, it could be strategically important to pitch so that you can demonstrate capability. This positioning – or, more accurately, prospect grooming – is often vital for new businesses or companies that are looking to develop longer-term sales opportunities.

Proposal strategy

Putting together a winning proposal demands time, energy, resources, enthusiasm, imagination and careful planning.

Whilst creativity is vital, thoroughness is equally important since it demonstrates that both your attitude and aptitude to undertake the requested contract are in place.

Teamwork is particularly important when it comes to preparing major pitches as it ensures that all avenues are covered.

In securing success, it's quite likely that you will need to orchestrate a broad mix of skills from across your business to discuss, explore and ensure a consensus of approach. Brainstorming this composite team can then explore:

- What key elements should be brought out in the pitch
- What the approach should be
- What technical inputs are needed
- Key differentiators
- Past experiences that could be brought to light
- Project team and structure

To do this well, a pitch leader should be appointed to co-ordinate the team's input to the document and drive the performance effectively.

The key responsibility of the business development function – in other words, you! – is to ensure that all the bases have been covered in terms of the offer to the prospect. If there are gaps in the knowledge base then further work is needed. Our

---

Creating a game plan – key components
- Understand the situation
- Find out more information if needed
- Discover your opponents
- Find out how pitches will be evaluated
- Be clear on the decision maker
- Attempt to establish the budget

...*Put these points together to work out **your** competitive advantage*

Whilst you can't judge the book by its cover, if the cover looks good and the contents in it create impact, then you've got a best seller

experience of working with successful pitching businesses demonstrates the importance of an aligned and thorough approach to cover the key elements shown in the box.

Proposal structure

Successful organizations make their offers 'look different'. Their proposals possess strong visual impact. Prospects look at many different proposals, and the reality is that it is the ones that catch their eye that will stand out.

Here are some ideas that are worth checking out:

Making your proposal stand out – eight ideas

1. Your cover could carry a visual element that is pertinent to the prospect's market or need

2. Use a solution driven message on the cover that sums up your offer

3. Consider a CD presentation of the contents of your proposal on the inside pocket of the pitch

4. Think about drawing together a one-page 'road map' of what the customer will get on the back of the front cover – an executive summary snapshot

5. Think about producing your proposal in a different shape or size, e.g. A5 or A3

6. A proposal presented as a newspaper or magazine might be an option, particularly in a fast moving market

7. Vary the way your proposals are bound or put together e.g. as a ring binder

8. Don't think that words are the only way of communicating your ideas; consider using a series of illustrations, or photographs to do the job

---

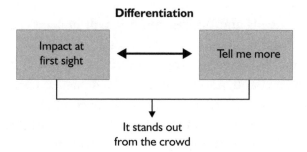

Differentiation

It stands out
from the crowd

Getting the content right

The second stage of the proposal structure is to ensure that what sits between the covers – not just how it looks but what it says – clearly meets the prospect's needs and budgets.

Let's just spend a moment considering the warning at the top of this section – don't cut and paste old stuff.

Because of the time and effort that needs to go into pitch preparation, the temptation to re-cycle is ever present. Whilst managing time is an integral part of your role, this should never be at the expense of freshness of thinking and writing winning pitches. It's an unpal- Always start with a blank sheet of paper atable truth, but using old pitch documents as the basis of new offers leads to complacency and lack of original thought and effort.

Whilst there are elements such as standard clauses or regu-latory information that can be pulled out of old pitch documents, we should never forget that:

- Clients' needs differ
- Budgets vary
- Individual personalities require different 'button pressing' techniques
- Contracts have different timescales and output require-ments

By starting with a blank piece of paper you start to focus on customers' needs and desires and this will in itself create a differentiated and targeted flow of thinking.

The most successful proposal writers treat each new pitch in a unique fashion, and this approach impacts enormously on conversion rates and wins. What sits between the covers of the pitch is driven by functional mastery skills – a lucid demonstration of what and how the offer will impact on the prospect's operations.

So, creativity and originality is key, but it doesn't stop you using a checklist of core components to ensure that you're covering all the critical ground within your presentations.

Here are some guidelines on what areas, issues and topics should be covered within the tender document that hits the target's desk:

Guidelines for Proposal Preparation and Contents

Key element	Think about covering	This demonstrates
Set the scene	• State who the customer is • Key background • Say how you will help	Personalization of the pitch
Understanding of customer need	• Provide an overview of current situation • Cite what the issues are • State the challenges and opportunities • Summarize what needs to be done	The challenge is clear, you understand them and their market and you know what they want
Objectives	• Provide an overview of the contract • Be clear on the key issues of the intervention • Break down the contract into individual deliverables	How you see their goals, and begin to construct how you will help them achieve these aims

Approach	• Provide a step by step approach • State how each of the methods you will employ will meet the objectives	How it will be done
Staffing	• Say who will do it • Provide résumés of staff • Highlight their expertise	Provides confidence in the quality of staff
Outputs	• Break down clearly what the customer gets as a result of you giving a product/service • Demonstrate tangible and intangible benefits	What the customer gets – actually and emotionally
Timescales	• When each element will be delivered • Critical delivery points • Milestones and review dates	Your ability to meet their requirements within a definable time plan
Credentials	• Similar contracts • Customers • Case Studies • Testimonials • Website links	Credibility and trust Evidence of capability
Fees/costings	• Fixed and direct costs • Extras – make them visible • 'No hidden surprises'	A return on customer investment
Regulatory	• Quality standards • Professional indemnity • Diversity policy • Company policy • Health & safety	Professionalism

REWIRE YOUR THINKING

New ideas, sparks of inspiration and fresh connections come to us all at some point. But so, unfortunately, do brick walls, dead ends and crossroads where we are not sure what to do, where to go or how to address a particular pitch.

Sparks of inspiration and brilliant ideas just seem to come naturally to some individuals.

Are they born with a new business pitch gift? Or can their skills be acquired through practice and rewiring our minds to think in more open and lateral ways?

There's no question that we all possess the seeds of creativity – the trick is to master careful cultivation to ensure that it grows and can be ultimately accessed to achieve a competitive advantage over our rivals who are all busy working away – quite possibly on the same piece of new business as ourselves!

Ground rules for re-wiring

A research paper published in Management Decision in 2000 (Elspeth McFadzean – Henley Management College) highlighted some of the common characteristics of great creative minds of our time.

The ground rules of great creative thinking

1. Develop a clear desire to win with specific goals in mind
2. Motivation, dedication and commitment should be the drivers of our work
3. Take risk and be prepared to fail – in other words, be brave
4. Make connections and observe relationships between all things
5. Learn, draw conclusions, and identify alternative strategies from failed projects/initiatives
6. View projects from different angles
7. Hard work must be followed by periods of relaxation
8. Follow your dreams
9. Conceptualize problems from novel perspectives
10. Work in groups to stimulate new thinking

What does this mean to you? Run down the list and ask yourself honestly – how many of these do *you* practise? If there are some that you've had to say no to – why? Then ask yourself – How can I reorganise my behaviour to take on board this new thinking? List the ones that you think are in greatest need of attention then think of ways to address the issue.

Coaching the mind to think differently is the starting point for this new way of thinking.

Use the library and make the connections

Paul Carroll, founder of PR consultancy Communique views his approach as his own 'mind's library' and that everything he sees is registered because one day he may need to retrieve the information. This kind of technique can be extremely powerful in the context of increasing your new business strike rate. This technique was viewed as the basis of the brilliance of Leonardo Da Vinci known as 'Connessione'. Da Vinci practised systems thinking which comprised a recognition and appreciation for the interconnections of the things and phenomena.

Practice the following to help you rewire

- Be constantly aware of what other companies – both from within and beyond your market – do to promote and sell their products and services
- Take time to review websites and brochures from non-related market areas. Challenge yourself to identify their key messages. Then ask yourself – Can I apply this approach to my business?
- Ask contacts and individuals you come across from other non competing areas to share concepts and techniques that generate prospects and win customers

As you practice this way of thinking your mind will start to make connections and slowly but surely it will happen for you – the ideas will come. When they do, the chances are that they will be directly relevant to your own personal selling situation or to a customer find, win or keep demand.

A golden rule

If you are going to make a big breakthrough then you have to do things differently. If you don't, then forget it!!

It is vital that you are not stuck in the past as the research tells us – many of us are!!

THE MIND GYM

If you're looking to exceed prospect and customer expectations, you need to work out how you can change your approach and rewire your thinking.

In a world that over the last ten years has been dominated by best in class practices our view at Strategem is that the world has to move on and start to think about best in class *different* practices.

Here's how you can get this edge – by thinking of your brain as a mind gym.

Put your thinking, the way that you approach things on the training circuit. Get used to the idea that you're going to become the supplier whose reputation is synonymous with startlingly effective solutions. Ideas come from individuals and teams, but we have to start with our own thoughts and mindset. The starting point for effective creative thinking is to think: *"Yes, I am creative and I **can** make a huge contribution to new ideas"*. Here are some of the exercises you can try as you enter the gym.

The mind gym

1. Allow yourself to *fantasize* about customer wins and possibilities. When you do this imagine how that success will feel as you secure that prestigious contract
2. Think about the *startlingly original ideas* for achieving new

lead generation, customer retention, personal brand building, and industry thought leadership status. Don't dismiss them, give them time to germinate

3. Put on the *'mental suit'* of someone you admire. Imagine you are that person in a meeting

4. Allow time to *daydream* during the day particularly mid morning and mid afternoon. These are the times when your mind will start to overload. No good ideas will emerge if you are stressed

5. If you've a big challenge ahead, get on your bike, or jump in the pool! Many of the best business development professionals we've encountered firmly believe that exercise helps them towards the solution they'd been seeking – especially where new ways of doing things are needed.

PRACTISING THE NEW WAYS

We looked in the section on Momentum on how to cut out routines that serve us badly as business developers. As we develop our concepts and prepare ourselves for the pitch, it's time to put into practice some of the well-known tools that help create new ideas and fresh approaches.

Here is a selection of some of the most useful ones.

Thunderbolting

You'll undoubtedly have come across brainstorming to generate good ideas. A strong concept, but perhaps too many people take too long coming up with too few new thoughts.

Where Thunderbolting differs is in its brevity. Thunderbolting sessions should last a maximum of 20 minutes and be conducted within an environment that is conducive to idea generation – *make it fun!*

Ground rules

■ Postpone your judgement

- Foster openness in the group
- Pay extra attention to naïve ideas
- No arrogance
- Hitch-hike on others' ideas

Run the session in teams of five or six. This should comprise a cross-section of people from a variety of functions in the business.

When you have your long list of ideas, group them and organize them into an ideas cube:

The Ideas Cube

Not feasible ideas	**"Forget it"**	**Yellow ideas** • Ideas for the future • Dreams/challenges • Stimulation for the brain • Red ideas for tomorrow
Feasible ideas	**Blue ideas** • Easy to implement • Few risks • High acceptability • Past examples available	**Red ideas** • Innovative designs • Breakthroughs • Exciting ideas • Can be implemented
	Known ideas	New ideas

Blue   = Go for it!
Red   = Will make a big impact
Yellow = May distract you short term

Ask the searching question

In coming up with creative solutions and answers to problems, you'll need to be able to ask pointed and searching questions.

If you are thunderbolting be clear to define the question for what you want ideas, because the first step towards solving a problem is by defining it.

Try a thunderbolt session with your colleagues around the following questions:

- How can we double our sales to customer X?
- How can we double our turnover next year?
- How can we sell £Xm of the new product?
- How can we improve our sales lead generation activities?
- How do we write more creative pitches?
- How can we make our presentations come alive?

Such pointed and open-ended questions should generate lots of new ideas. When you have thunderbolted these areas place your feedback in the ideas cube. Take action with the blues and the reds.

Asking the opposite (reversal)

This technique can be effectively used for improving the business development find, win, keep process. It works by asking the opposite of the question you want to ask. This might sound like a particularly odd concept, but it can really help you to view your business development challenges from a different perspective.

If we take the scenario of wanting to create a bigger impact at customer presentations we may wish to ask the question "How do we perform badly at the next customer pitch"?

Your answers would include:

- Don't bother making any initial contact
- Don't research the audience or understand the personalities
- Don't take any company information
- Produce a badly designed presentation
- Don't bother to research possible objections
- Forget the screen and projector
- Don't take any supporting samples
- Ignore past successes
- Forget handouts

Reversal techniques imply that if you do the opposite of what not to do, then this should produce a positive outcome.

Ask why?

This is a highly effective way of getting behind a particular issue.

Ask why? and we can often get to the root cause of a particular problem or issue. In raising questions, we not only give ourselves some of the answers, we can also map out the rationale for a strategy, or a series of tactics.

Here's a short example of how this technique could work.

Ask why?

Why did we miss our national sales target?

Although we exceeded in most of the country, we were well short in two key regions. This was because we didn't recruit sales people in the South West and North East early enough in the period to make a difference across the year.

Solution – invest in better HR and recruitment in field sales. Take remedial action sooner within a time period to ensure that targets can be met.

Businesses that ask themselves why, and are open and honest to positive self-criticism, are well on the way to becoming progressive, improving organizations. They're willing to challenge themselves, work on the root causes of failure, and creative and confident enough to put solutions in place.

Just in time probably isn't good enough – the majority of pitches and tenders must be submitted by deadlines stipulated by the client, and, obviously, if you're involved in a live presentation, well, it's not much good turning up one day late, or even one hour late.

Nevertheless, far too many organizations end up burning the midnight oil trying to get pitches out of the door to ensure that the documents arrive on time, or are still hassling their secretarial staff to make late adjustments to the slide package an hour after they should have left for the pitch.

It's clear that for many businesses, the final stages of the process are often the most time consuming because assembling the information, editing and proof reading are frequently time sapping.

So, what's the solution? Unfortunately, there are no magic bullets here; all you can do is recognize that there will always be this last minute dash for the tape, and the only way you can overcome this is to build extra breathing space into your schedule from the moment you get the green light to prepare the tender.

Ideally, complete the draft document at least a week before it is due to either be presented or to land on the target's desk. You'll then be able to:

- Add any additional information you think needs to be incorporated
- Enable all stakeholders of the project to have a final input
- Allow consensus to be reached on the content of final document submitted

Pitches that are written well within the timescale of the delivery date are usually the ones that are free from grammatical or typographical errors, omissions or oversights.

In other words there is a greater comfort factor – yours! – with pitches that are produced and prepared well in advance of their due date.

BRAVERY AND ITS ROLE

In business development we are often faced with difficult, awkward or intensely competitive situations. If it feels like that to you, it's probably going to feel the same way for the other companies that you're up against. In these situations, it's the operators who're big and brave

He who dares wins
SAS motto

enough to battle through the challenge that tend to emerge with the prizes.

These characteristics are even more important if there's a perception that you are coming from behind the pack – either because there is intense competition or there are a number of established suppliers. In these scenarios, there's only one strategy that can be pursued. You really have to take a different approach that stands above the rest; that gets noticed; and ultimately creates attention, interest and desire.

Practising bravery

Back in the pre-privatized days of the UK trains industry, the advertising agency Saatchi & Saatchi were asked to create a new promotional campaign that emphasized the organization's commitment to customer care. As many commuters and passengers will be aware, this was possibly not the company's strongest card to play.

How did Saatchi & Saatchi, who were up against a blue chip incumbent, play this one? Their approach was bold but ultimately very effective.

They kept senior officials of British Rail waiting in their reception for over half an hour. The client team were dealt with in a brusque manner by the agency's reception team and offered fairly cool coffee and a plate of rather tired pastries. Not, possibly, the best way you would think of treating such senior members of a potential customer. On the brink of leaving because of the apparently dreadful treatment they had received, the pitch team walked in and greeted the British Rail executives with the statement – "You know how it feels now".

This extremely courageous – and, it has to be said, creative – stand taken by the agency paid dividends. Saatchi & Saatchi secured the contract – precisely because they were brave enough to demonstrate customer connectivity and functional mastery in one imaginative step.

It is vital, though, not to confuse bravery and courageousness with stupidity; where you're looking to be is creating differentiation.

Practising scary strategies

The leading management guru, Rene Carayol, regularly talks about being scary. Within the concept and thinking of exercizing bravery and courage to win, Rene recommends that we consider *scary strategies*. These are methodologies that help lever competitive advantage from particularly difficult selling opportunities where there is an incumbent supplier that has been servicing a particular customer or market need for some length of time. Situations that need the deployment of a scary strategy may include:

- Pitching against global brands
- Bidding against competition that has held a contract for years
- Introducing new products to a traditional market
- Trying to sell an innovative concept or idea
- Building a commercial presence as a smaller unrecognized supplier competing against a blue chip supplier

In considering scary strategies we must think about:

- Challenging the status quo and encouraging the customer to change their perceptions
- Bringing a different and unconventional approach to solving the problem
- Challenge existing practices that are old fashioned, out dated and in need of a different approach

A definition of insanity
Doing things the way you have always done and expecting a different result.
Rene Carayol, management and transformation guru

- Taking an unorthodox approach that is well founded and based on knowledge and to the future benefit of others
- Using them when it appears that all other methods of winning business are failing – you have to do something different. Use the definition of insanity to help you change your thinking

As Saatchi & Saatchi ably demonstrated, a choosing a scary strategy can highlight your command of functional mastery. By flexing your product or service knowledge and understanding the market in which you operate you can clearly demonstrate that change is needed to improve the existing situation.

By implementing a courageous standpoint, customers will listen, because your ideas and concepts are based on lucid thinking.

A scary story!

A supplier of cladding boards to the local authority housing refurbishment sector was convinced that his company's new range was significantly more weather proof than those offered by his more established competitor.

So what did he do?

He invited senior architectural specifiers to a series of roadshows where, by placing each board in boiling water for the length of the presentation, and then inviting his guests to view the results afterwards, he in effect conducted a series of accelerated wearing tests, "right in front of their very eyes", as the show business saying goes.

Working on the assumption that seeing literally was believing, impressed architects, who could see that the new product survived in much better shape than the old solution, promptly switched their business to a relieved and very happy commercial director!

This could have gone massively wrong but he went for it!

This scary story is another example of playing brave and playing to win. It's not, perhaps, as sexy a case study as our British Rail example, but it shows clearly that you don't have to be in a "glamour" market to think outside the box.

You can use a *Thunderbolt* session to produce ideas to drive a scary strategy and encourage your team to do something different to get a positive result by shifting your prospect's perception of the status quo.

It can, of course, depend on horses for courses; all organizations will react differently to the approach you adopt – which is one of the reasons it's called a scary strategy!

Depending on your perception and research into the organizational mindset of your prospect, you should choose your tactics according to what you calculate would work best.

Using entertainment strategies to build personal relationships with customers	**Conservative organizations**
Adopt a strategy that is firmly rooted and clearly signposted into their commercial requirements	
Get your pitch endorsed by a world-leading expert	**Increasing scariness**
Team up with a global market player to enhance your offer to the customer	
Bring a 'world class' personality to a pitch situation	
Challenge your customers' way of doing things by well thought through thinking	**Forward thinking organizations**
Take an exciting customer to a presentation or pitch	
Tell customers they only have to pay if your product/service makes a difference	

Another way of thinking about scary strategies is breakthrough thinking and implementing new ways of getting the message across. The next time you feel that you are getting nowhere with a prospect or your pitches keep coming second think:

What scary strategy can I implement to win?

In other words, as we say elsewhere within the book, rewiring the way we think as business developers is a crucial element to breakthrough thinking.

HIGH IMPACT PRESENTATIONS

For many business developers, winning new contracts will involve personal presentations to the prospect.

Achieving the perfect pitch is an art and a science in itself, probably with an element of show business thrown in for good measure.

The first thing to say is that although you might not think so, it's no walk in the park for your client either.

The chances are that they will be devoting a couple of days to hearing presentations for significant tenders. They'll almost certainly be overdosing on coffee and tea, eaten too many biscuits, and, especially towards the end of the proceedings, may well have lost many of their powers of concentration.

They desperately want to be informed, and, it must be said educated *and* entertained, but their ability to differentiate between wall-to-wall promises becomes increasingly blunted. As most pitch audiences are drawn from a cross section of your prospect's organization, it's likely that they will possess different hot buttons from their colleagues, and some, it has to be said, could well be mutually incompatible.

Your job is to sparkle, communicate lucidly, and leave them with a smile on their face.

Are you still up for it?

If this sounds like an impossible mountain to climb, don't worry. It's never, perhaps as bad as that, and remember, you're in front of them to help them meet their targets, so you should always get a good reception, as most audiences recognize and remember this trade off.

To start with, let's highlight some essential points for you to remember.

High impact presenting – the ground rules
1. Be the 'inspired' you
2. Distil the key messages of the sales message
3. Know your audience
4. Make sure that you are fully prepared (functional mastery)
5. Make it both logical and creative – The Treasure Chest

The ability to prepare and deliver a presentation is at the core of the business development profession.

So, if you're part of the nervous majority, you're not alone! Follow these ground rules and your chances of creating a high impact presentation will dramatically increase your chances of success.

> A staggering 84 per cent of UK Directors rate public speaking as the most daunting business activity.
> *Aziz Management Communications Index*

1. Be the 'inspired' you

Most strong and experienced presenters will recommend that you should be yourself when giving presentations.

Whilst we don't disagree with this sentiment, it's also true that there are many versions of 'you'. What you really need in a sales situation is the *inspired* you – the performing star that captivates their audience with energy and passion. The inspired you sends clear signals that your offer is the only choice.

Where does the inspired you come from? Hard work, practice, patience and persistence are, in truth, the core ingredients of connecting with the inspired you, but you also need to search inside yourself to identify what creates the 'inspired you'.

We all have things that help us to reach for our own personal energizer; different things trigger different people, so it's vital that you use your energizer to ensure that you're ready to deliver an effective presentation.

This element of the sales process is concerned with momentum building skills that bring about motivation and positive attitude. Energizers that have been used by many of our clients over the years have included:

Energizing to find the 'inspired you'
1. Meditation
2. Listening to classical music
3. Solitude
4. How would my hero tackle this challenge?
5. Positive personal reaffirmation
6. Spiritual scriptures, emotional literature
7. Deep breathing
8. Exercise
9. Listening to motivational CDs, tapes or reading books that inspire
10. Phoning a friend

See how many of these unlock your mind, and douse the sparks of self-doubt?

Find your energizer and you will do away with negativity to ready you for the performance. Find your energizer and make it become a regular feature of your rehearsal for important sales presentations.

2. Distil the key messages

There's a good chance that your prospective customer may well have requested documents such as a tender or proposal for a given contract or piece of work before you actually present.

Don't assume that the audience will have read your document in detail because they probably won't have! What is vital is that you can distil clearly the messages of your offer. Your challenge on the day is to demonstrate:

- That you understand the current position or issue facing the client
- You have a solution to meet and exceed their needs and expectations

Once you are clear of what the key messages of the offer are, summarize them as bullet points. View your messages as important statements and tangible outcomes.

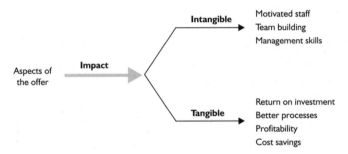

3. Know your audience
Before you go and make a presentation you should be clear about who is going to be there and why. Be sure that you know what message they want to hear and which buttons need pressing!

If you've done your job thoroughly then there should be no hidden surprises. Telephone your contact or the project leader two days before you present so there is total clarity concerning the audience's needs and issues.

4. Preparation
If you've mastered the functional mastery process you'll be totally clear about:

- Their environment and what drives them

- Why your products and services are the best
- How they are different and outperform the competition
- Why your organization is the best to deal with

You also need to ensure that you are very clear on what you are going to say and when, how you are going to say it, what examples and anecdotes you are using, and what kind of props you'll use.

The best presenters don't just mug their way through a presentation and do it brilliantly without any practice whatsoever. It really doesn't work like that for anyone. They spend hours mentally and physically preparing for sales presentations. In short, they take time to think it through and map out clearly the messages for the day.

5. Make it logical and creative – getting the right props

Advances in technology make it far too easy nowadays to put your audience through "death by Power Point". For some poor folk, it's only the caffeine in the coffee that keeps them awake!

It's therefore critical that you make your presentation informative and entertaining – although how you go about this will depend on the audience's personality, as well as the types of products or services you are offering.

Presentations should combine logic with creativity. What we should endeavour to identify before any presentation is the right "props" for the day. Your job is to leave your audience with:

- Something they'll remember
- Messages that they won't forget
- Props that make them sit up and listen

You might never get the chance to pitch for a wacky client like a radio station, but you can "think Treasure Chest" by asking yourself:

What's *your* treasure chest?

A PR Consultancy was invited to present for a client in the radio industry. It was likely that their audience would be turned on by a bold and imaginative pitch, but turned off by the traditional "chalk and talk from suits" approach that might have been considered.

So, conscious of the need to think differently, the consultancy dispensed with the laptop and, instead, bundled their presentation into a treasure chest!

A loaf of bread and a pat of butter to illustrate basics, and a jar of jam, to flag up extras, were then revealed to a bewitched panel.

The presenter then pulled out £50,000 in used £10 notes to highlight the budget; this final twist enabled them to walk away with the deal there and then.

"How am I going to make sure that this audience really remembers our presentation when they're making their decision?"

Samples, prototypes, full-scale models, a video, or a CD could all be on your presentation wish list.

What is vital and most important of all is introducing an element of appropriate quirkiness in the presentation that the client will remember.

As one client stated "when you get to the last presentation in the day you've seen five PowerPoint presentations and they all said more or less the same thing".

It's worth finding your treasure chest, because it means that you will be able to use a combination of communication methods are used – and mixing different techniques means that your message is more likely to be remembered by your target.

A combination of these approaches leads to a powerful and high impact presentation.

Finding the treasure chest

- A dramatic act to make a point or demonstrate an important client benefit?
- A clear, waffle-free approach to message dissemination?
- Music, sounds, words, pictures, actions, role-play?

We must aim to leave the presentation with the client thinking:

I really enjoyed that. It was different and exciting.

TEAM SELLING

There's a lot to be said for being a brave business developer. But it's also vital that you know when to call in the reinforcements.

Most professionals within this industry possess, to a lesser or greater extent, what might be termed the martyr syndrome – "I'm going to do this alone, because I can, because no one works harder than me, because no one knows the prospect as well as me, because…"

Sounds familiar?

And yet, the truth is, that martyrs fail more times than the business development professional who's willing and prepared to make each pitch a team game.

"If you're going on a pitch, you need to field a team"

All too often, business developers fail to make the sale because of a personal crusade to show that "they can go it alone", when in reality it's the end result 'win' for the company that is, of course, vital.

Team selling is not just about two business developers meeting an individual customer – this could often be misunderstood to be pressure selling. Rather, effective team selling occurs when other functions of the business are built into a selling situation.

This is especially important where more complex solutions are needed. Quite often the business developers who act as the hunters can only go so far in answering technical questions and providing functional mastery; their true skill lies in recognizing when to bring in other expert colleagues. In this respect, team selling underlines the clear intention of a business to support, assist and communicate different possibilities.

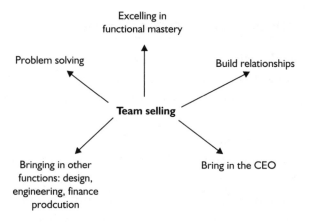

What can add further weight to the selling function is when your most senior person – your CEO or equivalent – becomes highly visible in the business development process. This adds credibility and completes the functional mastery loop, as CEO visibility is a commitment that an organization's competencies, experiences and resources will be brought to bear in a given contract or tendering opportunity.

A battle is often won by a combination of land, air and sea efforts
John Leach

The team approach also proves to be an effective mechanism in Customer Connectivity in a number of broader circumstances.

- All people possess different personalities, so our chances of engaging with a prospective customer is increased if we're able to broaden the basis of our relationships

- This healthy mix of skills can be used at different points of the connectivity process

Key tip
In the interests of making the sale, be sure to bring in the appropriate expertise when and when it is required

In the team selling process the secret is to understand where and when such interventions are needed.

GETTING THE BEST DEAL – CLOSE THAT DOOR!

Consultative selling requires persistence, perseverance and patience. All well and good, but, as most of us know, real life isn't always that forgiving, and the majority of business development professionals understand the importance of keeping a smooth flow of new contracts.

This can often put the focus on accelerating the pace at which some negotiations are concluded, so that you can either bring the date on which the contract is confirmed, or, if the target customer ultimately decides to look elsewhere, you're not left with a growing list of "hot prospects" of which you're increasingly uncertain.

So, if a prospect is on the hook, how should you play the line to land the fish?

1. Don't sacrifice profits for turnover
Do you think customers in buying situations that require consultative selling buy on the cheapest price or the best added value for money? It's an easy question to answer, isn't it?

Don't grab at business. If, in your anxiousness to close a deal you compromise your margin you may well end up cutting the ground from beneath your feet and make the newly formed relationship impossible to fund, and impossible to service.

Explain very clearly to the customer that quality is an important element to your quotation and offer, illustrate differentiation and added value, in term of the people, skills, materials and technical capability. Bring these components into the negotiation.

2.   Strike the right balance

We believe that the best customer–supplier relationships occur where there is a positive mutual respect and regard for each others' sovereignty.

Suppliers that roll over to a client may well seem impressive initially, but in the long term, they don't necessarily help themselves or their customer. Make sure that your prospect understands that you're eager for their business, but also ensure that they realize that you'll make a strong partner, not a subservient junior who won't act effectively.

3.   Make your prospect feel special

All customers need to feel that they are getting good value for their investment. It's your responsibility throughout your negotiations to ensure that they know that they will enjoy this return from you – and that they feel that they are a special case. This can be useful to accelerate negotiations, as it plays on the emotional drivers of the customer.

4.   Look for a different way

There's rarely only one way of doing a job, and seldom is there only one price.

If your recommendations and costs are blocked at the first hurdle, ask whether you can re-engineer your offer to meet their budgetary needs and requirements. Exploring these alternatives can often lead to a diluted version of the original quotation, but by proposing other possibilities then a win could be achieved. This is common in complex selling situations – put forward alternatives in your quotation. Build it up as a modular package where additional extras are costed separately.

5.   Build in flexibility

Being able to maximize the margins in any contract is vital. If you aim too low then you'll probably not have given yourself enough room for manoeuvre, especially if your customer wishes to negotiate. Make sure that you have allowed yourself enough space in your profitability calculations to accommodate some movement.

6. It's a team game

Negotiations invariably involve other functions and teams within your business. Incorporate the skills of your colleagues in finance, marketing, engineering, design, technical and so on – they will be able to broaden your understanding of what's possible and where costs can and cannot be compromised.

You may also wish to use other team members to conclude negotiations and secure the contract and the costing. If you pursue this strategy, ensure that you've reviewed and agreed the negotiation points and make certain that all members of the team are fully aware of their role and input.

7. Ask the tough questions

At some point of the win process it will be down to you to ask the question: "Have we got the order?" Few of us enjoy being so bold with such a bald question.

But look at it this way. You've put a lot of time, energy and effort into solving their problems.

In many ways they owe it to you to be honest with the answer. You've actually earned the right to ask it, so start to think more positively about it!

There are a number of different ways you can ask the question, including:

- When do you think you'll be making a decision?
- Are there any reasons why we won't be able to work together?
- We would like to do business with you – do you feel the same way about us?

- Is there any more information you need from us before we can start?

Just ask!

8. Negotiate from a position of strength

If you've followed our guidelines and suggestions, then your functional mastery linked to your customer connectivity skills should have made a clear imprint on the consciousness of the prospect. In other words:

- You've shown them that you understand their market and their need
- You've clearly demonstrated that you, your company and product/service can address the need
- You've communicated why your offer is special

Rolling these issues into one means that you are on the front foot and not on the defence.

Think about it like this: it could well be that they need you more than you need them!

Without this being a recipe for arrogance, we think that's quite a powerful and positive thought to possess.

You should aim to infuse your negotiations with the poise and serenity that confidence in your solutions should bring.

... & WHAT DO YOU DO IF YOU LOSE?

This book is all about winning, but life is enriched by setbacks as well as successes. If you miss out on a deal, yes, you can get hung up on the "show me a good loser and I'll show you a loser" cliché.

Our advice is to forget this sentiment and consider that failure can often be the

> If you fall off your bike get back on and pedal faster
> *Frank Dick*

starting point of a turnaround. If you get a rejection, do your homework and be professional about it.

If you do lose then be sure to:

- Let the customer know that you are disappointed
- Ask why you missed out – get under the skin of the reasons
- Ask when there will be another opportunity – or ask if there are other immediate opportunities
- Visit for a full briefing
- Write back to the customer in a positive light – wishing them success

Few business relationships are cast in stone, and if you impress the customer as you withdraw gracefully, it's our experience that you are often in the best possible position to pick up the work next time it comes up for re-pitch.

Similarly, thorough and honest feedback from a rejection can often help you evolve – or transform – your solutions, which can have a hugely significant and positive impact on your business. Experiencing the pain of failure is an excellent recipe for getting it right next time.

Feel the pain of losing but turn it into a positive.
Learn from the reasons.

WINNING THE BUSINESS – A CHECKLIST

- Winning business means selling yourself, your offer and your company
- Keep in mind at what stage you're up to on the Connectivity Spectrum
- Your first date is important; make sure you look and act the part
- New prospects need to believe you and believe in you

- Attract attention, interest, and desire to win the order
- Don't be a busy fool – your time is money
- Understand what you need to know and plan your questions prior to a meeting
- Practise your listening skills
- Use mind mapping to take notes – it really works
- Master objections by prevention rather than cure
- Be patient – complex sales often incorporate a significant gestation period
- Make sure your pitches are not "me too"
- Avoid re-cycling old proposals in the hope they'll fit – they usually don't
- Think scary!
- When you're pitching – dare to be different
- Find the treasure chest that suits you and your audience
- Think team, and your chance of winning will be significantly enhanced
- Use the eight golden rules of closing the deal!

CHAPTER 9

Keeping the Business

All successful company leaders will tell you that building long-term relationships with customers is at the heart of their success, particularly as finding new business costs far more than servicing existing relationships.

Keeping your customer, however, isn't just down to selling and customer relationship management; it also relies on how well your business as a whole

> There is nothing more deceptive than the obvious fact
> *Sir Arthur Conan Doyle*

meets and exceeds the expectations of the clients on its book. Although the hard work of winning a new account should never be underestimated, it's also true that once you've won a contract the *real* hard work starts towards building an effective partnership that reaps long-term rewards for both buyer and seller. It's also a fact that businesses are failing to capitalize on customers they have already.

Maintaining a high quality service should be a prerequisite. It's also about producing the right products and services that are delivered on time every time.

How many of you are already musing "Well, that's not my job – that's down to production, or engineering, or sales admin and processing, or R&D"?

In some ways, that's fair comment, but the reality is that as the eyes and ears of the business in the market, it falls within your reach to drive forward new ideas,

> **We are not capitalizing on our existing customers!**
> A recent survey showed that 6 out of 7 businesses are failing to capitalise on their customer base
> *Colin Coulson-Thomas, Professor of Competitiveness at Luton University*

better working practices, products and service developments that meet the aspirations of the customers you all share.

These ideas and new possibilities emerge as you develop your relationships – and the truth is, building strong relationships with clients matters more now than it ever has done.

Why? Given the impact of supply chain rationalization and globalization, many major customers are looking to deal with fewer and better supplies, rather than the tens, hundreds, and in some cases thousands that were commonplace up to the 1980's and 1990's. The message must be: once you have secured the customer, do all you can to keep them.

A 'keep' strategy encompasses:

An evolutionary relationship

Relationship ──────────▶ Partnership ──────────▶ Total integration

Too many businesses work tirelessly to secure a contract, ply their "new best friends" with the best service they can muster, then, once the honeymoon period is over slip down the slope of giving less and less attention.

As you start to develop your keep strategy you must consider how relationships and partnerships evolve.

Remember that Future figures highly in our 4Fs rule. But it's not just your future we're talking about – it's there's too. In any analysis, what's good for them is good for you, and vice versa. This concept of balance and mutual benefit is at the heart of building long-term relationships.

You'll want to make a profit; they'll want a high quality service. Somewhere out there is a compromise position where both partners are happy. The suppliers and customers who strike this balance are the ones that ultimately win in the long term.

In thinking about an effective model for Keep Strategies, relationships can be viewed as:

'Keep' strategy

BUILDING THE ACCOUNT: SEED, GROW, FLOURISH

Seed, grow and flourish. The first order has been served and there is evidently long term potential in the account you have just acquired. The key from here is to ensure that you maximize the relationship potential and grow the account to the optimum levels for your company. Here, what's key is not to over-stretch or over-commit, particularly in the first few months of a relationship. Getting too greedy at an early stage can often end up in an untimely end to a relationship.

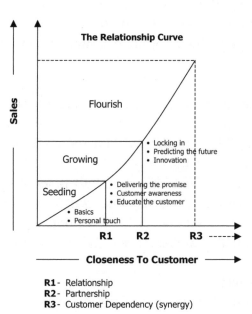

The Relationship Curve

R1 - Relationship
R2 - Partnership
R3 - Customer Dependency (synergy)

We can use the relationship centre to view how to grow sales from our existing customers.

SEEDING: GETTING THE BASICS RIGHT

Bedding in a new account is vital and, as all good gardeners know, seedlings needs careful nurturing in those early stages of development.

Nurturing a new customer

New customer integration processes need to be put in place when a new contract is secured. The starting point is to remove any potential barriers from the new relationship. Are you easy to do business with? Your efforts should be channelled to ensure an effective gateway for customers to access the resources, products and services you promised as part of the winning process.

Start by:

- Returning all calls made by the customer
- Don't over-complicate things
- Be clear on any potential pitfalls
- Quash any problems or unnecessary systems from the contract

Over-cumbersome processes can damage satisfaction levels in the early days of a relationship. If this is the case then these processes should be eradicated and replaced with more customer friendly interactions.

Remember too that importing best practice from the way that you deal with existing customers will form the blueprint for your new contract, but that all client relationships will be subtly different, so intelligent flexibility is the key to success.

The personal touch

Building rapport not only with your immediate contact but also with their team is an important element within newly formed relationships. If you take the trouble to learn more about the individual's personal circumstances, interests and aspirations you will start to equip yourself with some of the knowledge that could be key to building the longer term relationships needed to grow the account. At the end of the day doing business with people we like makes life far easier and more enjoyable, especially if it is built on a basis of trust and credibility.

GROWING: MAXIMIZING THE OPPORTUNITIES

Delivering the promise

Delighting customers really means exceeding their expectations. You can most simply achieve this not only by ensuring that your customer feels involved but also by going the extra mile and providing an extra that they didn't expect. Delivering the promise is also about beating deadlines, generating a stream of new ideas, and providing input that does not always carry a price tag.

Ensuring customers are fully aware – don't miss opportunities

There can often be a tendency to assume that your customers are totally aware of the full range of services offered by you. This is a common mistake made by many businesses.

All too often companies become aware that their customers are sourcing products and services from alternative suppliers that could have been serviced by you!

Educate your customer

You can overcome this by ensuring that your customer is fully conversant with the full spectrum of your products and services.

A cost-effective way of doing this can be implemented by inviting your customers to your premises or staging customer awareness days where the full complement of the services offered are presented in a structured 'soft sell' way.

These activities promote an ideal way to raise awareness of the broader capability of your capability to your customers. An informal setting can also begin to forge close working relationships.

FLOURISHING: FROM PARTNERSHIP TO SYNERGY

Locking in

Aligned to growing an account is a mechanism put into place so that you can ensure that your business is delivering added value to your customer. Locking In is the process of getting close to the customer so that a competitor faces an almost impossible task to dislodge you.

Lock Ins can be secured by:

- Locating staff on the customers premises to service a contract or job
- Providing added value technical, research and development or production support
- Investing in plant and machinery resources on behalf of a customer's need

Predicting the future

By working closely with customers, it's possible to predict and anticipate potential problems or opportunities before they're even aware of them. In moving towards a relationship based on partnership an ability to spot customer challenges through functional mastery – in other words understanding of the market and industry dynamics – is vital.

Customer dependency

An ability to problem solve and see what is coming up places a supplier in a powerful commercial position, as it can lead to customer reliance and further strengthening of the partnership. An incumbent that has provided such a "value adding" strategy will be tough for even the best competitor to dislodge.

Innovation

Most clients value proactive input that an imaginative, commercially sophisticated supplier can bring. As your business development function identifies client issues and challenges, you should then set to work to offer solutions.

At this stage ideas papers can be created, or customer/supplier workshops can be staged to scope out the scenario as you see it, together with potential remedies. By matching a need with a solution, you stand a significant chance of success not only in strengthening your relationship with your client but also in maximizing profitable sales.

CULTIVATING THE FUTURE

Because the ways in which customers choose to work with their suppliers are changing rapidly, today's business developer must sit even closer to the customer. Anticipating changes in needs, building relationships, and forming synergetic co-operative arrangements are all driving imperatives for the business developer.

Functional mastery skills will need constant updating and improvement; this goes not only for the Steady Eddies amongst us, as we aspire to be Winners, but also for the Winners themselves!

In achieving long term working relationships with customers the prizes include:

- Increased customer profitability
- Lower costs of sales
- Further customer dependency
- Lower vulnerability to client loss
- Reduced marketing costs
- Better and more effective planning of operational resources to match a clearly defined forward workload
- High degrees of credibility in the market place

. . . So the prizes are worth having, but you've got to invest the time and resources to make this happen – as well as ensure that a commitment to building relationships comes right from the top of your organization.

Team-based relationship development is an integral part of the success of this process. All your key functions should be committed to working with their opposite numbers within the client organization; they should also be encouraged to work together to ensure that the quality of the support you're providing is consistently high.

COMMUNICATION

Our experience has shown us that breakdowns in communication are a major cause of losing business and customers.

If your communications skills are poor, it can limit your understanding of the way in which your customer's needs, challenges and problems ebb and flow.

Make sure that you plan your communications effectively. Who is talking to whom? Who are your delegated members of staff at meetings? Have you created a customer relationship management process – usually, although not exclusively, on a computer – to enable your team members to keep a record of communications, track changes, and act as prompt for further activity?

By discussing and communicating at all levels you'll get to know what's going on – both at a professional and emotional level. It's also important that you and your team understand the culture, language and politics of your client's business.

This will help you individually and collectively to avoid silly mistakes that can demonstrate to a client – "they don't really know us very well, do they?"

> "These guys have spent the last two years as suppliers working for the Co-op, and yet they always insist on calling us a company, when we're actually a society. I know it's only a small point, but it really annoys my directors, and it

Spread the net of customer contacts

One of our clients recently told us that they considered it sufficient simply to deal with one person – the engineering director – of a major customer.

Much to their surprise a highly lucrative contract was awarded to one of their key competitors. Although many of the company's contracts were routed through their main contact, on this occasion their customer chose to involve other specialists in the specification decision.

Our client lost out – simply because they had neglected to form relationships with other decision makers in their customer's business.

The lesson to be learnt here is that the pressure point matrix doesn't just apply when you're building relationships with a prospect; it continues to be valuable when you secured their business. The client in this case ignored the design team that were working on a new idea that carried the significant contract.

shows us that they've not spent the time learning about the movement's history at all."

It's critically important that you treat these "soft" aspects of your client's background, and the way they work together, with respect. You can then begin to anticipate:

- The difference between what the client says and what they really mean
- What's in their history and heritage that makes them think, say and do what they do
- Where the weak links are in the customer's team
- How the key relationships are formed between their team members and whether there are any personality clashes
- Where the political pressure points lie

This information is vital as you begin to prioritize the best ways of approaching the individuals in the customer's business. In doing this, you should also anticipate then avoid the pitfall of getting "too close" to certain individuals as other members of the customer team can receive this very negatively.

Remember

1. Communication applies at all levels and within all specialisms of the customer's team
2. Don't get too close to any one member of the customer team
3. Understand the customer's culture through discussions at all levels
4. The passives can provide valuable information
5. Understand the professional, political and emotional drivers of the team
6. Constantly add value by bringing new and innovative ideas to the table

---

In earlier chapters, we've talked about delegation and the need for you to avoid the martyr syndrome.

An effective customer relationship management process helps you steer round this potential pitfall. It's simply not feasible, if you are primarily responsible for your organization's business development process, to stay at the forefront of all customer relationships, particularly as you become increasingly successful in winning new work. It's straightforward to keep in with, for example, three existing customers, while pitching to win 10 more. But what happens if you win all 10? You aren't going to be able to keep in with 13 and chase for a further 10, and so on.

Ultimately, the introduction of a customer relationship management process gives you and your business the opportunity to shift primary responsibilities to colleagues. You may still be involved to a certain level, but this process, if implemented professionally, allows for a seamless transfer without disrupting your client's perception of the buying experience, and enables you to continue to concentrate on what you do best – business development.

PARTNERSHIPS AND ALLIANCES

Forging alliances with other businesses is becoming an important element of sales development and customer retention.

Mergers and acquisitions are expensive to secure, time consuming to construct, and are by no means assured of success. Informal partnerships, however, can be forged relatively quickly and cost-effectively, and can enable participating businesses to expand their commercial horizons profitably.

Successful partnerships can help in:

- Tackling new markets
- Growing critical mass
- Adding value to existing customers
- Satisfying a need identified in the market place that could not be tackled individually
- Raising customer perceptions of what you can offer

Over the years we have worked with a multitude of clients that have formed both formal and informal alliances to bring momentum to the customer offer. Typical examples include:

- Estate agents teaming up with major house builders
- Interior design companies teaming up with office furniture manufacturers
- Economic planning consultants forming alliances with building surveyors
- Legal and accounting practices creating alliances

Extending the offer through partnerships

An associate of ours had been providing technical support services to a group of biotechnology start-up businesses. The project was being funded by a major Government business support agency. A new initiative was being considered by their client, it focused on assisting the same group of businesses to construct business plans that would be used to raise finance from venture capitalists and high street banks. The company was keen to bid for the work and whilst they had some expertise in this area they lacked the management, financial and marketing expertise to secure the contract. There approach was to team up with ourselves and an accountancy practice to offer a complete package. Their bid was accepted, they extended their offer and whilst they had to share the contract they won more business from an existing client. It would have been easy for them to say we cant do it. A little bit of lateral thinking, however led to more business.

- A consortium of building products manufacturers and design specialists creating off-the-shelf packages for architects

Such complementary skills bring a new dimension to the critical mass of an offer that can be made to a customer. In creating such alliances the decision to go ahead is often outside the scope of one individual; more often than not it is a move that is sanctioned at board level. Whilst this may be the case, the driving force and need for such an alliance often originates within the sales, marketing and business development function. In the identification of potential partners and alliances it is vital that collaboration is set against the background of the following considerations:

The sum of the parts are greater than the whole
Anon.

- Both parties have a common vision
- The partnership/alliance is customer focused
- They possess a shared set of values and operating principles
- There is familiarity and integration across both parties' organizations
- Both parties share a culture of risk taking, bravery and implementation of scary strategies
- Visible symbols of trust and collaboration can be created

Above all, alliances and partnerships must be customer focused. It is an area that brings with it a wide range of new possibilities and new learning experiences for both parties – and, indeed, the customer. Access to partners and alliances provides the 'bolt on' capability and access to resource that satisfies customer needs.

Like failed mergers, however, some alliances can go wrong. Typically alliances that start out with good intentions fail because:

- The ground rules of the relationship are not clear
- One of the parties gets greedy
- Lack of business to justify the partnership's existence
- Insufficient co-operation and communication
- Roles and responsibilities unclear
- The joint offer was not clearly defined

The task here is to be open with prospective alliance partners about the possibility of failure. A technique to use to help minimize this risk is to review each point here and ask "In what circumstances can we see this scenario occurring, and what preventative measures can we put in place *now* to stop this scenario happening?"

The opportunity to explore the benefits of creating alliances and partnerships is a powerful motivator, as they offer the

Alliances – simple checklist of questions

1. Is the customer buying products/services from others that if an alliance with another company was formed then a need could be satisfied?
2. Are there trends in our customers' marketplace that means we need to team up with others to satisfy demand?
3. How could alliances benefit our company in retaining and growing our market share?
4. What complementary skills within our industry align with our activities?

chance of mapping and matching new solutions to new problems and needs – now and in the future.

THE ROLE OF TRUST

Trust is key to forging and sustaining healthy commercial relationships. Our promises and offers to clients face their ultimate test in the actions that we take to deliver what has been agreed.

Whilst misunderstandings occur, these can be forgiven if they are genuine and based on poor or insufficient communication. These instances become apparent very quickly and more often than not can be resolved without any further complication.

It almost goes without saying that losing trust can be very damaging. As relationships build, the trust element gathers pace and one of the most difficult jobs for business developers is rapidly gaining customer confidence and trust. It's also true that although it can take a long time to build a trusting relationship it takes a lot less time to lose it! Once trust has been lost, it's a long road to recovery. Examples of how trust can be made visible include:

- Returning telephone calls and emails promptly

- Listen to customer concerns then act upon them
- Documents are made available within a timescale promised
- A problem is solved or an alternative solution is provided to a customer's challenge
- Products and services are delivered on time
- Saying 'no' when you can't meet a request

When starting to build trust these simple rules apply:

- Speak the truth as much as you are able
- Reliability – do always what you say you will
- Testimonials – provide 'proof of source'

KEEP THE BUSINESS – A CHECKLIST

- Keeping existing business and winning more sales from your current clients is far easier than securing new clients
- Aim to move relationships, from the initial phase, through to partnership, through to total customer integration. This way customers become dependent upon you
- Ensure you integrate new clients consistently thoroughly through their 'seedling' phase
- Nurture new customers by reviewing any potential barriers to growth – remove any unnecessary processes and make it easy to do business with you
- The personal touch is vital not just with your immediate customer contact but also with the rest of the team
- Go the extra mile and give customers something they weren't expecting
- Don't assume customers know everything about you – and vice versa
- Sit close to customers so they are fully aware of what you offer and so you can predict future needs
- Constantly create and feed in new ideas for trial

- Team selling is vital in keeping business – include other parts of your company in the process
- Ensure that there is effective communication with your customers. Hold education and learning days
- Assess where partnerships and alliances can bring 'added value' to your relationship with customers
- Trust underpins 'keep' strategies

PITCH PERFECT – PULLING IT TOGETHER

CHAPTER 10

Managing the Find, Win, Keep Process

Pulling customer connectivity together means that a process has to be put in place that coordinates, monitors and reviews the success of the find, win, keep activities. The core components of a SMART management system should include:

S Sales plan – what, why, who, when, where
M Monitoring of sales and prospects
A Account planning
R Records – keep accurate and up to date customer details
T Track performance management

CREATING THE SALES PLAN

The sales plan lies at the heart of the business development function. It should be fully aligned with the enterprise strategy for your business. The sales plan provides you with a clear route map that will show you how your targets for the organisation will be achieved.

The plan should clearly define:

- Core deliverables
  - Sales targets
  - Targets by customer/account
  - Target by region
  - Budgets (generation of leads, brochures, website, etc.)

- Key customer/account plans
- Key projects including new product launches, new markets, market intelligence
- Controls and measures

GUIDING PRINCIPLES

Managing customer information in a structured way is vitally important for any business developer. Over the last few years we've seen an increase in Prospect Acquisition Management tools to assist the business developer to target their effort effectively.

These tools help to collect data from all channels:

Market research	Field sales
Records	Internet
Marketing campaigns	Telephone, fax, email enquiries

Many busy entrepreneurial businesses thrive on fast-paced activity, and there's a natural tendency to decry neat and tidy minds, possessed, say the entrepreneur, by desk flying bureaucrats.

The trouble is, that a degree of tidiness *is* a prerequisite of managing prospect acquisitions effectively. After all, information is often lodged in people's heads, on their desks, on their PCs and on scraps of paper, when in truth, it's really only useful when incorporated into one place. As with all such tools, however, Prospect Acquisition Management needs quality human inputs, as what you get out is highly dependant on what you put in.

Putting in place an effective Prospect Acquisition Management process can bring some or all of the following benefits:

- Better insight and strategic awareness
- Helps leverage more from existing customers
- Brings focus to lead generation, qualification and follow up

- Ensures that we are tracking whether budgets are being met
- Better early warning systems to highlight potential short-falls/problems
- Builds our awareness of the need to put in place activity today for new sales tomorrow

Clearly, if you're not familiar with a process like this, it's going to take you some time and effort to develop, implement then fine-tune such a technique. This can be even more problematic if your natural inclination is to be an active "doer" and less of a planner.

Nevertheless, persistence with learning to master this process will pay dividends, so it's worth thinking through how you can make this work for you and your organisation. You may wish to consider delegating the creation and maintenance of your Prospect Acquisition Management process to other colleagues who might be better suited to make this happen.

There's a further area in which a better understanding and management of the prospect acquisition process can reap benefits, and that's in the control of your marketing and advertising budgets.

Only when you understand how your market works, and how the dialogue between your business and the prospective customers operates, can you make sensible choices about how you invest your budgets in this area.

Brochures, websites, advertisements, promotional items, magazines, newsletters, photography, PR – all come at a cost, and unless you understand and can measure the merits of each technique, it's almost impossible to say whether or not they represent good value for money.

So ask yourself the question – are the costs expended on business development giving you the return in terms of sales that you'd expected? Chapter 11 will help you to stay focused and ensure the activities being employed provide the necessary rewards.

Here we will now go onto look at some basic tools that will help you to manage the find, win, keep process. They will assist you in assessing whether you are on target to win.

KEY CUSTOMER ACCOUNT PLANS

Getting organized centres on having the key information you need at your fingertips.

By now, you should have a clear idea of the type of customer your want to do business with, and applying the 4F's rule – ensuring that wherever possible, your targets will bring fun, fame, fortune and future into your lives – will help guide you with this decision.

Your challenge is to assemble the core information and commercial intelligence on the prospect that you'll need to make a serious attempt on converting them into customers. While it's true that more complex target organisations will require time and effort to collate this level of detail, the return on your investment should you be successful will more than justify the commitment you make at this stage.

To guide your efforts in putting together a comprehensive plan for targeting a customer or account that has high potential, the issues shown in the account plan checklist (see next page) need to be considered.

By setting out a clearly defined method of attack the structure of your approach will yield far better results than merely just trying to 'mug' your way in. Well thought target account plans yield results. The structured approach can also deliver other benefits:

- You gather all the necessary background information that will help you in the sell
- Other marketing/communication tools required to be successful are integrated into the process

Key customer account plan: a checklist

Target Customer: _____

Contact Details: _____
_____
_____
_____

Organisational Links: _____
e.g. overseas/UK subsidiaries, related companies etc)

Website: _____

Key Documents:
Brochures
Annual Reports
Financial Accounts
Organisational Charts
Press Articles

Key Decision Makers: Yes   No
Pressure Point Matrix Complete   ☐   ☐
(if 'Yes' attach it)

Key Purchasing Data/Information: _____
_____
_____

Targeted Sales: £value _____

Key Account Plans (should include):

1. _____ (Who will be targeted)

2. _____ (How will the approach be made)

3. _____ (What is the offer)

4. _____ (Key milestones)

5. _____ (Primary business development tools to be used)

6. _____ (Other marketing support needed e.g. PR, advertising etc)

- Your target customer recognizes that you're taking a structured approach

THE SALES PIPELINE FUNNEL

How long is your sales pipeline?

Listen to what the marketing director of a leading UK kitchen manufacturer and retailer had to say about his customers.

> The average British kitchen is changed every eight years. The female within the home leads the purchasing decision, although it is usually the male that sanctions the trans-

action. She will start to consider options 18 months before the actual purchase is made, usually by buying home interest magazines. At this stage, it's important that our ads and PR are seen in these titles. She will use these publications to entice her partner into recognizing how shabby her current kitchen is, and how good, in contrast, new ones look. At nine months out she will visit showrooms on her own to build her own intelligence and shortlist her favourites. At four to six months, she will bring her partner with her, and begin to counter any of his objections. At three months, they will be in definite purchase mode, so our job is to make sure that at this and the two previous stages we've done our best to impress her and win him over too. We can then move to convert the sale and land the contract.

Wow!

Whether you agree with the somewhat traditional view of the role of the couple, you have to say that this guy knows his stuff – and how acutely aware he is, not only of the sales pipeline, but how, over time, these opportunities funnel into an actual decision.

Notice, too, how well he understands the purchasing cycle of his industry, and absolutely critically, he recognizes that winning an order in two years' time means choosing the right designs *now* to manufacture, photograph and promote ready for the prospect's evaluation in six months time…

How well do you know *your* sales funnel pipeline?

If we take the analogy of the sales pipeline, then we can start to visualize what needs to be done in order to secure customers.

Feeding the funnel – pipeline activities

Our activities in customer building techniques act as the pipeline to feed the funnel. A whole host of techniques need to be employed in order to generate those leads and contacts that may, if we work hard, become customers.

Sales funnel pipeline

SALES WIN!!!!

- *Position 6 – Prospect emerges:* Contacts and potential customers enter the pipeline when it becomes very clear that an individual has or may have a budget for a particular initiative or project. At this point it is vital that the lead and contact becomes visible in the sales recording process.
- *Position 5 – Positive contact:* At this point further investigations have revealed that an interest in the product or service you are offering may meet a potential customer demand. Telephone research, email dialogue has concluded that this project is real.
- *Position 4 – Face to face:* It is unlikely a sale will have taken place until face-to-face discussions have been initiated – this is fact!

At this point credentials have been made real and clear. A potential initiative or project is being discussed and all the idea generation and problem solving activities kick in. This pro-

In consultative selling, going from position 4 to position 3 can take a long time!

cess can, as we have already discussed, take a long time to move through because at this point a 'toing and froing' of correspondence, ideas papers, outline suggestions are the norm in consultative selling.

- *Position 3 – Costed proposal:* This is the point where a formal quotation or proposal has to be submitted.
- *Position 2 – Best few:* Probably a pitch or formal presentation is requested at this point. It is time to ensure that you have covered the ground, thought about all possible objections and that the best team is fielded to 'pull the order through'.
- *Position 1 – Win:* Time to ensure that the new customer is integrated effectively into your customer care programme and that the deal is constructed within the best long-term interests of both you and your new client.

This concept can be translated into a simple spreadsheet format where a sales value and its potential are attributed to each position. This helps to clarify whether you're putting sufficient effort into both feeding the funnel through your pipeline activity and whether enough effort is generating costed proposals. Positions 3 and 1 are the most vital points, however, if nothing is happening or the cupboard is empty at position 6, then you should start to worry!

A representation of the funnel in a simple Excel spreadsheet proves to be a more than adequate way of monitoring and tracking the find, win, keep process (an example of this approach is given on the next page).

This is a simple yet highly effective technique. Remember if you don't have enough quotes at position 3, you will never reach the sales target. Maintaining a healthy pipeline is crucial to any business success.

Prospect No. and Desciption	Date	Account Manager	Number in Pipeline										
			Value								£	£	£	
			Deadline	Prospect Emerges 6	Positive Contact 5	Face to Face 4	Costed Proposal 3	Best Few 2	Sales Win 1	Cost	Not Proceeding

	£value	No.
Total Bids (period under review)		
Total Sales		
Conversion Rates		
Live Quotes		
Sales Lost		

Sales Target	
Total Sales	
%	
Balance to Sell	

Period Under Review:

VISIT REPORTS

Accurate prospect intelligence is at the heart of making sensible decisions on customer acquisition, retention and profitability.

A commitment to gather and record prospect intelligence will enable you to plan well, spot trends and ultimately provide the right products and services to meet current and future demands.

The business development function is the primary feeder for any enterprise strategy, and customer information is the basis upon which we plan our future strategies.

Recording customer feedback, thoughts, views and ideas will help you predict:

- Future needs
- Current dissatisfaction
- Potential problems
- Product improvement
- New possibilities

. . . but – we know, we know, compiling reports week after week is so *dull*!

Well, tough! No one said every element of your role would be exciting, yet, look at this task from a different perspective – reports can produce the nuggets that lead to exciting new possibilities. Regular visit reports should be done and distributed so that your business understands where its future profitability is going to come from. Don't just go through the motions and log them, half-heartedly into your prospect acquisition database; email the reports to relevant contacts in your organisation and discuss them – take action. A simple template for the visit report might look like this:

Visit Report Template

Organization:	Contact: Position:	Date:
Address: Tel:	Email: Website:	
Meeting Objective:		
Areas Discussed:		
Outputs:		
Follow Up Action: Notes for other colleagues:	Circulate:	

Like many other elements of business development, it's relatively straightforward stuff; the *real* challenge is to possess the stamina and discipline to put the processes in place and make them work in the long term.

VISUAL MANAGEMENT

If you drive down a road and see a traffic light change from green, through amber, to red, you stop (hopefully!). You don't need to read an instruction manual or have the concept and consequences of road safety to take action; the point has been communicated to you – quickly and successfully.

Communicating visually – through simple bar charts, line graphs or colour-coded systems – can be highly beneficial inn monitoring the sales process. Here are some examples:

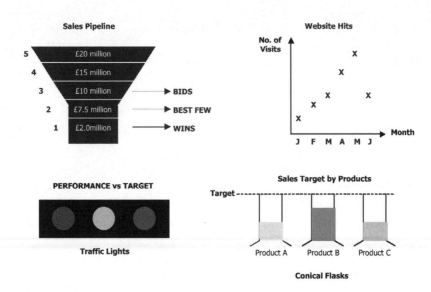

By distilling reams and reams of paper to one diagram it becomes very clear what kind of action should be taken next. The traffic light system depicting green as 'fine', amber as 'think about the situation' and red as 'sort it out' have been valuable tools to depict the status across a whole series of functions. So remember to make it visual if you want things to happen!

CHAPTER II

Staying Focused

So now we have looked at all the components of successful selling. The next challenge is putting it all into practice.

There are, of course, plenty of programmes, books and seminars out there that offer the Quick Fix. We're not sure that they really work. We think that true improvements in business development skills only come when the techniques become practised and the new ways of working become good habits. This all takes time, but, after all, sustainability is what really matters.

Things which matter most, must never be at the mercy of things which matter least
Goethe

This means that you should be committed to continuous improvement if you are to achieve and sustain peak performance. Remember, things aren't always going to go well every day; there *will* be times when you think you're losing focus and direction, and there are bound to be times when new business success isn't coming easily. By setting out very clearly what we want to achieve then aligning our actions to achieve our goals, it's far more likely that in the long run we will get where we want to be, and we will become more resilient to the bumps and knocks that life pushes onto us.

Our next challenge is to build a plan that will support us as we seek sustained selling success.

The method outlined is based on a corporate planning tool known as Hoshin Kanri. As the name suggests, this framework for strategic prioritization was originally created in Japan, and its basic concepts have been successfully implemented with many of our clients.

SELECTING AND SETTING BREAKTHROUGH GOALS

If you could write down a handful of commercial objectives that you would like to achieve, what would you prioritize? Of all the activities that we pursue, which are the ones that make a clear difference to the development of our business?

These are tougher questions to answer than you might first think. Often the glaringly obvious things we need to do get overlooked for some pet project that makes no impact on success. Time after time, business development professionals, in our experience, continue down the same path and set the same goals that yield average performance.

Why does this happen?

Lack of direction is often the result of trying to do too many things. We spread ourselves too thinly by taking on many different tasks and so fail to give those activities that will yield the biggest results enough energy and expertise.

However laudable multi-tasking is, real winners are able to prioritize and focus, and can often appear quite ruthless in their willingness to abandon those activities that they have predetermined will not deliver results.

To match their skills, we have to focus on the few vital goals that will make a difference.

In developing your own 'winner' strategy you should aim to set a maximum of three to four breakthrough goals.

Finding the breakthroughs will require conscious effort to truly define them and bring a high degree of clarity.

Some examples of breakthrough goals could be:

Breakthrough goals – some examples

- Break into two new export markets
- Increase sales to existing customers by 50%
- Identify and win £2.0m from two new customers
- Achieve 50% conversion on new business
- Become Sales Director within 12 months
- Become a leading authority in the market
- Introduce a sales management system that provide quality information
- Exceed my sales target by 60%

As we've said before, once you've defined your goals, you must commit them to writing. In doing so, you'll mentally sign a contract with yourself to achieve what you set out to do.

So, we know what we want to attain – we're being **S**pecific. We'll know whether we've attained it or not – it's **M**easurable. It actually fits within the context of our business – it's **R**elevant. . . . and it's going to be delivered within an appropriate period – there's a **T**imescale.

So it seems like this technique is a good old-fashioned SMART objective.

Well, not quite. Notice how we've left out **A**chievable? In our view, we'd rather use the word **A**mbitious.

There's little point in setting goals that aren't going to stretch your performance. If a goal is achievable, why bother setting it – we need to *stretch* to our limits and think about breakthrough.

MAKING OUR GOALS COME ALIVE

Once the goals have been set, the next step is to identify those projects that we need to deliver so that we can make them come to life.

This is where you can really see the concepts of functional mastery, customer connectivity and momentum in action, because we can develop responses to each criterion that contribute to moving us towards success.

To give you a flavour of how this might work, we've taken four of the breakthrough examples we've already highlighted, and drilled down to a series possible projects that we should consider as we strive towards our goals. The conclusion to this may look something like the table shown on the next page.

The next stage of the process is to be brutal and review which of the ideas will make the vital contribution to achieving the breakthrough.

As we start this review, there's an important piece of advice.

If you look at the worked example, you might think that they are all relevant. You're probably right, but this isn't the point! There aren't enough hours in the day to do all these things; and, critically, some will be far more relevant and effective than others to achieve success.

- In *Functional Mastery* you may be an expert already, so there would be no need to waste time going out with colleagues. Neither do you have the time to write articles. Perhaps what is needed is more product training and a better understanding of your competitors and what differentiates you, your product and your companies
- In *Customer Connectivity* you may not have the necessary resources to initiate regular mailings or attend more networking events. Perhaps you need to focus on being more creative with your pitches or paying more attention to the quality.

An example – breaking down the goals: level I

Breakthrough goals	Supporting projects that may contribute to goal achievement		
	Functional mastery	Customer connectivity	Momentum
1. Increase sales to my existing customers by 50%	• Write papers to go into leading industry journals	• Visit existing customers more frequently	• Building reputation in the market
2. Find two new customers and sell £BIG of new business for new product (Y)	• Build portfolio of how new product (X) works in practice	• Improve quality of tenders	• Use skills of colleagues
	• Understand what competitors are doing	• Be more creative in presentations	• React quicker to enquiries
3. Become leading authority in my industry	• Get better understanding of my companies skills	• Develop new ideas for existing customers	• Reflect more on success & failure
4. Improve my conversion rate to 60%	• Go on product training	• Plot pressure points for new customers	• Become a positive thinker
	• Accompany more senior staff	• Build key account plans	• Buy motivational tapes
	• Visit all major industry exhibitions	• Become more confident in presentations	• Reinforce my personal brand
	• Attend problem solving training	• Attend presentation training	• Sort my life out
	• Be the voice of the industry	• Use sales lead generation company	

Prioritize and transfer selected projects to winning framework

- In *Momentum Building* less procrastination and being speedier in getting back to customers may be the real breakthrough action. You may be a good team worker already, so spending more time with them is perhaps not needed. Conversely, you might need to build your personal brand and sell yourself better.

Take yourself through this type of questioning with a view to getting down to business and focusing on what will make the impact.

CREATING A WINNING FRAMEWORK

You should have now decided which projects will have the desired impact on your breakthrough goals. A plan of attack now needs to be constructed that makes the connection of project ideas with breakthrough goals. These projects will take you to your final destination. Display your plan as shown on the next page.

Alignment of breakthrough goals

Stars (*) highlight strong connections. Where there are gaps or empty boxes this means there is little or no connection between the project and the goal. If your plan has lots of empty boxes or circles (0) then you have to redirect your alignment. The plan above shows that there is complete dovetailing of the projects with the Breakthrough Goals.

Measures and targets

Each project must have a measure and a target; remember, what gets measured gets done. If you can't measure it, then you must consider whether it is worth doing. Some areas are difficult to measure but you must identify a way of putting some form of quantifiable assessment to it. The worked example provides some pointers to how you can do this.

Breakthrough Goals/Projects

		Functional Mastery				Customer Connectivity					Momentum				
		P1	P2	P3	P4	P5	P6	P7	P8	P9	P10	P11	P12	P13	P14
		Get Product Training	Build 'Real' Stories	Build Competitor Knowledge	Master Problem Solving Techniques	Improve Lead Generation	Put More Ideas Into Existing Customers	Increase Existing Customer Customer Visits	Build Key Account Plans	More Creative Presentations	Develop My Personal Brand	Develop Increased Levels of Motivation	Become More Of A Team Player	Clarify My Vision & Values	Think Like A Winner
Vital Few	VF1 50% increase in sales to existing customers	*	*	*	*	*	*	*	*	*	*	*	*	*	*
	VF2 Find 2 new customers and sell £BIG	*	*	*	*	*	O	O	*	*	*	*	*	*	*
	VF3 Achieve leading authority status	*	*	*	*	O	O	*	O	*	*	*	*	*	*
	VF4 Improve conversion rate to 60%	*	*	*	*	*	*	*	*	*	*	*	*	*	*
	Measure	3 Workshops with Senior Management	Complete *** Case Studies (10)	Profiled in Detail Top 10 Competitors	Attend 2 Briefing Session Mastered 3 Techniques	10 Qualified Prospects Per Month	5 Ideas Generated with Budgets	Monthly Visits to Top 5 Customers	Completed for all Existing & Potential Customers	3 Treasure Chests Identified and Delivered	Personal Brand Profile Mapped	Practice the 7 Laws of Self Motivation	Prepare 3 Bids with Support from Colleagues	Written Plan	Delete That Programme Practiced
	Target	By Dec	By Jan	By Feb	By March	September	October	Ongoing from December	By Jan	By April	May	Fully Operational by April	By Nov	By Oct	Onoing from NOW!
	Performance RAG														

Legend

* Completely Relevant
O Contributes
☐ (Empty) No relationship

Performance RAG

This stands for **R**ed, **A**mber, **G**reen. Make your plan visible. If project targets are being delivered then you can give this the green light. If you're moving towards it, you'll sign amber, and if you're falling short, you'll flag up a red. If your plans are covered in green then the breakthroughs are moving closer. If it's red, review your plan of action. Are you doing the right things?

Performance should be reviewed on a monthly basis to check whether you are red, green or amber.

ACTION PLANNING

Your vital projects carry a series of actions necessary for successful implementation. This drilling down brings a high degree of clarity to doing the right things. Such an approach, if carried out systematically, will improve your time management skills because everything you do moves you towards your objective and within a desired timeframe.

Drilling down to the next level involves taking each project and thinking through exactly what activities need to be instigated. A project sheet should be constructed for each project. A worked example for *P5 – Improved Lead Generation* is shown:

Level 2 – Project Action Plan
P5 – Improved Lead Generation
Measure: 10 Qualified Prospects Per Month
Target: Achieved by September

Action and activities	By when	Supported by
1. Purchased database material	1 November	Team members and other relevant functions. Tell them what you are doing!
2. Check contact list from 1.	22 November	
3. Find contact names (previous point)	30 November	
4. Attend monthly trade association event	ongoing	

5. Go through old business   2 November
   cards

6. Follow up press and   30 October
   advertising leads

7. Enter into email dialogue ongoing
   with contacts from 3.

8. Put creative letter   2 December
   together

9. Send out letter and   4 January
   brochure

10. Follow up 1 week after   11 January
    sending

Process of actions 1–10 means that by September a system will have been established

Such detailed planning needs to be applied to each of the chosen projects. The number of projects should never exceed 10–15 as this could result in overload.

The process of project activity can be extremely thought provoking. You may well find that it prompts you to consider:

- The detail of what needs to be carried out
- What activities are important
- What activities are not important
- Gaps in resources
- Support and team input
- Timescales and deadlines

It may take some time to get accustomed to this way of working, but in time you will build up a clear appreciation of the key personal and professional development issues that you and your organization should be addressing, both at strategic and tactical levels.

Use your plan as a reference guide for what is and what is not important within your activities, and, if reviewed on a regular basis, it should open your mind to new ideas and possibilities.

CHAPTER 12

Call to Arms

The world is becoming an increasingly competitive place to do business in. At a time when entrepreneurship and enterprise development is being encouraged by governments throughout the world, it is our belief that many companies are still spending too much time navel gazing into how they improve internal efficiencies and lean their operations.

To succeed, balancing internal enhancements, product development and quality with a culture that focuses on customers, markets and selling is vital. Providing individuals with the tools to effectively find, win and keep customers must be closely linked to an individual achieving personal peak performance. Acquiring the interpersonal skills necessary to build trust, and ultimately create win–win relationships between customer and supplier should be high on the agenda. All forward thinking and ambitious companies must practice this ethos.

In an era that will be further dominated by electronic transactions, businesses should not loose sight of the fact that selling is still significantly dependent upon human interaction. We should not let technology short-circuit the need for long-lasting relationships; it should be used to enhance them to the mutual benefit of both parties.

Customers are becoming more discerning and suppliers are being turned away if they can't demonstrate and articulate clear competitive advantage. This trend has given birth to the new age sales person – that person is a problem solver and consultant. A complete new set of new skills for the order winning process.

Those businesses and individuals that fail to recognize the

rapid changes taking place will pale into insignificance and find themselves as market observers. They will be left wondering what happened and why they have gone into decline. A sad story but reality for businesses of all shapes, sizes and maturity that don't sit up and listen.

This book is a call to arms for business people to rewire their thinking and encourage a sales culture that will fuel entrepreneurial growth. By approaching opportunities with freshness, boldness and a high degree of creative professionalism, businesses will achieve quantum leaps in sales performance.

The principles detailed in *Pitch Perfect* provide the starting point for individuals wanting to embrace the exciting opportunities that exist. By bringing together some practical selling concepts with creative new approaches to enhance your personal development, you will become prepared for the new selling age.

We want to see you and your business achieve "Winner Status". We want to see you implement innovative practices that will create balanced customer portfolios. Embed the *Pitch Perfect* themes into your behaviour and you will reap the rewards of customers that provide you and your business with fame, a future, fun and profit.

We are passionate about the role of selling and we want you to be tomorrow's corporate stars. Keep us informed of your progress and let us know how you are performing. Feel the impact of a winning sales approach!

Afterword

Thank you for buying this book. We are confident that when you incorporate *Pitch Perfect* principles into your personal and company practices, success will be just around the corner

It would be a very good idea to visit the *Pitch Perfect* website, which you'll find at www.pitch-perfect.biz

It's our firm belief that you can never stop learning, and the internet provides a fantastic opportunity for you to continue to improve your skills.

By registering at the site, you'll be able to obtain our latest views on sales and business development. We'll also be publishing a series of case studies and fact sheets that will continually refresh your commercial thinking.

Plus, you'll be able to interact, pose questions, and join in debates – and make *Pitch Perfect* a part of your professional life.

We look forward to hearing from you!

John Leach and John Moon

How Are You Peforming?

Mastering the Three Principles of Selling Success
A Step Closer to Becoming a Winner

FUNCTIONAL MASTERY

Rate yourself on a scale of **1–5** (1 Totally Disagree, 5 Totally Agree)

		1	2	3	4	5
1	I am clear about my company's strategy and vision	☐	☐	☐	☐	☐
2	The values that my company display are clear to the customer	☐	☐	☐	☐	☐
3	I can talk authoritatively about the resources available in my company (plant, design, people skills etc)	☐	☐	☐	☐	☐
4	I can talk in-depth about the products and services we offer and the benefits they bring	☐	☐	☐	☐	☐
5	I have an excellent understanding of the technical, commercial and market trends/issues that affects my customers sector	☐	☐	☐	☐	☐
6	I have a detailed understanding of the competitors offer	☐	☐	☐	☐	☐
7	Competitors' websites, promotional and technical materials are regularly reviewed	☐	☐	☐	☐	☐
8	I am clear about what differentiates my company's offer from the competition	☐	☐	☐	☐	☐
9	I have the tools to make our offer 'real'	☐	☐	☐	☐	☐
10	I build close links with other technical and commercial disciplines in my company	☐	☐	☐	☐	☐

		1	2	3	4	5
11	My customers trust my technical and commercial judgement and advice	☐	☐	☐	☐	☐
12	I have a clear plan for improving my knowledge of the products and services my company offers	☐	☐	☐	☐	☐
13	I can learn a lot from people in my business and my industry. I have a number of role models that inspire my judgement	☐	☐	☐	☐	☐
14	I want to be recognized as an industry expert and I do the appropriate things to make this happen	☐	☐	☐	☐	☐
15	I am competent at providing solutions to customers problems	☐	☐	☐	☐	☐

Score ___ out of 75

___%

CUSTOMER CONNECTIVITY

Rate yourself on a scale of **1–5** (1 Totally Disagree, 5 Totally Agree)

		1	2	3	4	5
1	We have a clearly defined enterprise strategy for our company (targets, products and markets to be targeted)	☐	☐	☐	☐	☐
2	I understand clearly the nature and structure of my company's market place	☐	☐	☐	☐	☐
3	I have a clear plan for finding customers	☐	☐	☐	☐	☐
4	My company has a clear picture of the customers we want to do business with	☐	☐	☐	☐	☐
5	For our target customers I clearly understand the nature of the decision making procedures	☐	☐	☐	☐	☐
6	Personal networking is a primary component of generating leads	☐	☐	☐	☐	☐
7	A structured approach is taken to understanding the buyer behaviour and pattern of my customers	☐	☐	☐	☐	☐

		1	2	3	4	5
8	A proactive programme of sales lead generation is instigated in my company	☐	☐	☐	☐	☐
9	Creativity is threaded through our finding and winning customer processes	☐	☐	☐	☐	☐
10	A structured approach to filtering the quality of the leads we generate is always instigated	☐	☐	☐	☐	☐
11	Time is spent researching the characteristics and personalities of the buyers we target and we always prepare	☐	☐	☐	☐	☐
12	I always gather as much information on a customer prior to any meeting, particularly first dates	☐	☐	☐	☐	☐
13	I prepare a list of questions that will be asked at sales meetings	☐	☐	☐	☐	☐
14	I am happy to ask uncomfortable questions when it is needed	☐	☐	☐	☐	☐
15	I am a good listener and I always take notes	☐	☐	☐	☐	☐
16	I am prepared for the likely objections that the customer will raise	☐	☐	☐	☐	☐
17	Meetings with customers are always followed up with an action plan or ideas paper or suggestion for next steps	☐	☐	☐	☐	☐
18	I can write comprehensive and well thought through proposals	☐	☐	☐	☐	☐
19	I understand the tendering and pitching process for my company	☐	☐	☐	☐	☐
20	I always try to practice with new ideas	☐	☐	☐	☐	☐
21	I am a great presenter and can articulate my company's offer to customers very closely	☐	☐	☐	☐	☐
22	I consider myself as brave when it comes to highly competitive situations	☐	☐	☐	☐	☐
23	I will ask colleagues to accompany me to important pitches	☐	☐	☐	☐	☐
24	I am a good negotiator and I know when to ask for the order	☐	☐	☐	☐	☐
25	I have built excellent relationships with my customers	☐	☐	☐	☐	☐

		1	2	3	4	5
26	Winning a new customer is only the start. I employ all the necessary activities to ensure we generate more business and keep the customer happy	☐	☐	☐	☐	☐
27	We hold customer education and networking events	☐	☐	☐	☐	☐
28	We build relationships with our customer at all levels and we are always coming up with new ideas	☐	☐	☐	☐	☐
29	We have a network of associates and partners that we can offer our customers to provide added value	☐	☐	☐	☐	☐
30	Our customers trust me and my company	☐	☐	☐	☐	☐

Score ___ out of 150

___%

MOMENTUM

Rate yourself on a scale of **1–5** (1 Totally Disagree, 5 Totally Agree)

		1	2	3	4	5
1	I view myself to be a winner	☐	☐	☐	☐	☐
2	I always try to stay positive and I think in a positive way	☐	☐	☐	☐	☐
3	My life is well balanced and I regularly take time out	☐	☐	☐	☐	☐
4	I am clear about my ambitions and what I want to achieve in life	☐	☐	☐	☐	☐
5	I am clear about my personal values	☐	☐	☐	☐	☐
6	I have taken time to cultivate my personal brand	☐	☐	☐	☐	☐
7	I take full responsibility for my life. It's down to me to make it happen	☐	☐	☐	☐	☐
8	I keep myself motivated and when under pressure I can cope	☐	☐	☐	☐	☐
9	I am self confident	☐	☐	☐	☐	☐
10	When it comes to making decisions I always act fast	☐	☐	☐	☐	☐
11	I am a team player and call for help when it is needed	☐	☐	☐	☐	☐
12	I always push my comfort zones to the limit	☐	☐	☐	☐	☐

		1	2	3	4	5
13	I constantly strive for new ways of doing things	☐	☐	☐	☐	☐
14	I have a good reputation in the industry and my market place	☐	☐	☐	☐	☐
15	I always celebrate success then move on to the next challenge	☐	☐	☐	☐	☐

Score ___ out of 75

___%

LOOK AT THE WHEEL

SCORES   %

Functional Mastery

Customer Connectivity

Momentum

Now plot your percentage on the wheel.

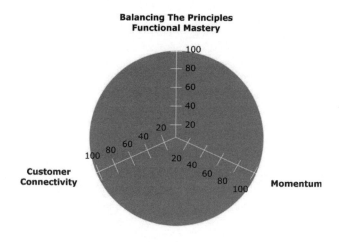

Balancing The Principles
Functional Mastery

Repeat this process every three months.

Index